Like Father, Like Son

INTRODUCTION BY

Robert Fulghum

G. P. PUTNAM'S SONS
New York

Like Father, Like Son

Hunter S. Fulghum

G. P. Putnam's Sons
Publishers Since 1838
200 Madison Avenue
New York, NY 10016

Copyright © 1996 by Hunter Samuel Fulghum
Published by arrangement with Hunter S. Fulghum
and becker&mayer!
Library of Congress Cataloging-in-Publication Data
Fulghum, Hunter S. (Hunter Samuel)
Like father, like son / by Hunter S. Fulghum.
p.   cm.
ISBN 0-399-14142-1
1. Family—United States—Anecdotes. 2. Father and
child—United States—Anecdotes. 3. Fathers—
United States—Anecdotes.
I. Title.
HQ536.F94   1996   95-47693 CIP
306.874'2—dc20

Printed in the United States of America
1   3   5   7   9   10   8   6   4   2
This book is printed on acid-free paper. ∞

Book design by Marysarah Quinn

To the Old Man,
JB, and the Toad,
with Love

Acknowledgments

To Jim Becker, Andy Mayer, Barbara Rodriguez, and the crew at becker&mayer!, Elizabeth Beier, Barry Neville, Donna Gould, Lisa Miscione, and Emily Sommerfield, and the people at The Putnam Berkley Group for all their efforts in transforming an idea into a finished book;

To my family and friends for their support and encouragement;

To Marie, my wife, for her love, feedback, and patience, especially on those days when I spent more time with the word processor than with her;

But most especially to Samantha Becker and Sarah Fulghum, without whose friendship this book would not have come to pass;

My warmest and deepest thanks.

Contents

Introduction

Once upon a time, there was a child called Sam.

At age five he was enrolled in a preschool class, which met in the education wing of a large church. Sam was one of those kids teachers called "strollers." Because they were independent-minded and tended to wander off on their own adventures.

One October afternoon, Sam detoured from his class as they were headed out the door to the play yard. He roamed down the hall and into the foyer of the women's restroom, where the school art supplies were stored. Rummaging through the cabinets, he found a five-pound box of red glitter. Which he tossed in handfuls on himself, the foyer, and the women's restroom. Like the sugar-plum fairy, he danced down the hall casting glitter as he went. On into the offices of the school director he skipped, shouting as he made his glittering entrance, "YOU KNOW WHAT? YOU KNOW WHAT? THERE'S CHRISTMAS IN THE BATHROOM!"

Sam's father liked hearing that story. He told it on several important occasions, making the point that Christmas is where you look for it—and may be found almost anywhere if you have the open eyes of a child—even in October in a bathroom. One is free to make one's own celebrations of life.

It was said in the family that Sam had "funny brains."

Over the years, many Sam stories accumulated in the family scrapbook. All his life he's continued to live in an open-eyed and open-minded way. His father appreciates this, because when the father was a child, his family said he had "funny brains" for the same reasons. Like father, like son.

When Sam was a teenager, he collected his father's favorite stories and had them printed into a small book entitled *Christmas Friarworks,* and he gave it to his father. A memorable gift. Sam was his father's first publisher. The text included a story called "Christmas in the Bathroom."

Sam is a father now. He has a five-year-old son named Max. The genetic thread continues: Max is another "stroller" with "funny brains." Like father, like son.

But I will not tell you any Max stories.

I pass that pleasure on to Hunter Samuel McClellan Fulghum, who is the author of his own book—this one. Once upon a time he was that kid called Sam. As his father, I am pleased to notice that he still has "funny brains."

ROBERT FULGHUM
Moab, Utah

Like Father, Like Son

Bite

The boys were digging for pirate gold. A cairn of cobbles—nuggets of gold, they claimed—was piled up precariously close to the largest of their pits. Every now and then, Max or Billy or Adrian would scramble from the hole with another rock clutched in one hand to his chest and his shovel held in the other hand. Watching this exercise made me cringe as I considered the probability that if the boy slipped, he'd sooner go down than drop either the rock or the tool, and like as not, he would land chin first on the shovel. I could picture the split skin and the buckets of blood, the trip to the doctor to have it stitched up. An image to make one shudder.

But little boys have the sure-footedness that comes from a low center of gravity. The "nuggets" were deposited with a satisfying dull plonk on the growing pile.

Returning to the pit, they dug enthusiastically, flinging sand in all directions. Their efficiency was poor—maybe a quarter of a cup of soil actually made it out of the hole each time, whereas at least ten times that slipped back in to the hole—but in their enthusiasm they did not notice, and they jabbered back and forth as they labored.

"Wow! We got a lot of gold!" said one.

"Yeah, now we can buy a super jet plane," replied the second.

"I get to steer first," added the third, and at this a disagreement erupted over who gets to drive first, second, and third. Tempers and voices were rising toward an ugly crescendo of, "I'm not your friend anymore!" when one of them, in a uncharacteristic moment of rational thought, suggested that they will take turns driving the plane, shooting the guns, and bombing the bad guys. No order was decided, but the suggestion seemed to calm them down enough to get back at the business at hand, the continued search for "Blackbird's Treasure." (I have tried to explain to Max that the pirate was named Blackbeard, but he has indelibly written Blackbird in his brain, and it isn't worth the effort to correct him.)

If you knew me as a small child, it wouldn't take you very long to figure out which one of this trio is mine. The smallest of the three, Max, is also the dirtiest and wildest, dumping more dirt down his rubber boots than anywhere else.

I left him to his digging for a moment longer while I collected his lunch box and backpack from his cubby. Just above the cubby, there was a folded piece of paper with my name on it. A note from the school's director.

I was to be advised, the note explained, that Max was not nice today, that he bit another child on the arm, and while the child was screaming, Max followed up with a right cross to the child's other arm. I was to understand that this sort of behavior is frowned upon, particularly the biting, and would I please discuss this issue with Max. Thank you and have a nice day. A large happy face adorned the bottom of the page.

Driving home, I considered how best to deal with the situation. The thought of sitting the boy down after watching him have such a wonderful time with his buddies, to have one of those father-son-you-shouldn't-do-that-next-time-use-your-words-not-your-fists chats was less than agreeable. I hate to burst his bubble and end an otherwise good day on a sour note. But I had to agree with the teacher. Biting is bad.

After dinner, I shooed the rest of the family away, and Max and I sat down. The child knew quite well that this is an immediate tip-off to a lecture or punishment and he stared at the tips of his sneakers and twiddled his fingers, shifting nervously every few seconds.

"Max, you got in trouble today?"

"Yeah, I did, and I got in trouble and had a time-out and got sent to the office. And teacher was mad at me."

"Do you know why you got in trouble?"

"Yeah." He wasn't going to confess. Not yet.

"Max, your teacher says that you hit Ben. And you bit him. You know we don't do that."

"Yeah, I did. I bit Ben and then I hit him." He was still looking down, now a little forlorn. "But I had to!" he said, lifting his gaze straight at me, his eyes not wavering even a bit.

"Why, Max? Why did you have to bite him?"

"'Cause he was hurting Katie, and I didn't like that! I tried to tell teacher, but she was busy and didn't listen! So I bit Ben an' hit him, and he stopped hurting Katie. And then teacher got mad 'cause I bit Ben, and I got a time-out!"

In all the world, Katie is Max's best friend; the two of them have been buddies for almost five years. Max is small, but Katie is tiny, and she is apt to be run over by some of the older children. My son decided to do the gallant thing and take the bully down.

This presented a dilemma. On the one hand, I disapprove of hitting on general principles, and any parent you'd care to ask would tell you how bad a bite can be, especially if it breaks the skin. And I have been trying to get him to understand that it is best to use words to settle a dispute. Or to walk away from the confrontation. I want him to know that throwing a punch is absolutely the wrong way to settle a problem.

On the other hand, it warms my heart to know that Max was brave enough to step into a situation where a smaller child was being picked on, even though Max himself was smaller than the fellow he took on. There is a sense of fearlessness and gallantry in the situation that appeals to me. The world needs people who aren't afraid of a fight, verbal or otherwise. And in a certain corner of my brain, considering the size difference between Max and Ben, I was secretly very pleased that Max had won.

I struggled with the right fatherly thing to say. I really want my child to learn to settle issues without resorting to violence. I really want him not to be afraid of a bully. These goals do not seem to work together very well, especially when you're explaining them to a five-year-old, a child who thinks that rocks dug from a sandbox are nuggets of gold buried by the Pirate Blackbird.

I pondered on it for a bit, with Max watching me, waiting for the reprimand.

What I wanted to tell him was that there was much about the episode that made me proud. I admired his bravery. And that while I was unhappy about the fight, especially the biting, it was balanced by his reasons. In effect, what I needed to tell him was that I was far from unhappy with him, but I felt an obligation, as a responsible adult, to tell him that he had done something bad. My problem was that I didn't want him to get the wrong message. Finally I decided.

"Max, you are having a five-minute time-out that started four and a half minutes ago. Sit here and count to thirty. Then you can go."

He looked at me, puzzled. He understood that he had been in trouble. So why wasn't I really punishing him?

"Daddy, are you mad at me?"

"No, honey. But next time, don't bite."

Dinosaurs

There is a spot in southeastern Utah where the rocks have been weathered by millions of years of wind and rain and cold and heat. In more recent memory, jeep tires have contributed to the wear. In the most worn-down place, a dull greenish band of rock—the Morrison layer—has been exposed. Scattered along the edge, where the green rock and the layers above it meet, you can see dinosaurs' tracks.

Hundreds, perhaps thousands of them, meander along the boundary, showing where some of the beasts walked, looking for food or water or mates, or perhaps just wandering. Ancient sauropods wading in a shallow lake, leaving behind reminders that they, too, passed this way.

I spent a morning tracing these steps, completely caught up in the excitement of each moment. My father and I called to each other as we found new sets of prints. And as the afternoon approached, we sat down on a rock that bore the rippled imprint of an ancient shore, smoking cigars and watching a thunderstorm rumble across the valley. From where we sat, we could watch semi-trucks, dinosaurs of a different kind, as they roared down the highway that cuts through the rocky country, from Crescent Junction and Interstate 70 south towards Arizona. Fifty feet away, some small shards of flint lay just beneath a rocky outcrop, detritus of the passage of the Indians who once lived here.

Sitting on that ancient rock with my father, I had a moment of connection. Behind me were traces of long-lost thunder lizards, who lived and died when I was only a trace of a gene within the cells of small, frightened mammals. Among the rocks were the bits of chert and flint, the garbage and leavings of my more recent relatives. And in my hand, a fine cigar from Sumatra smoldered in a cloud of blue smoke, a bit like the thick exhaust of the distant trucks.

My father and I—and the remnants of past lives—watched the passing of the day with the busy truckers and tourists and felt for one instant an awareness of the larger span of the universe.

We spoke of the past and the future. My father talked about my grandfather, a man I never knew. He told me stories about growing up in Texas, riding horses, being my age in a different time and place. He grew up never imagining that the world would come to where it is today, and he knew that the world would take my son places that neither of us could begin to fathom.

Somewhere in the stories, there was a sense of his handing me the past, not just of his life, but of all the things and creatures that had come before—the dinosaurs, the Indians, the father, and the grandfather. All of them converge, for now in some measure, in me, in the twisting path that is our history and heritage. My own children have taken the leading edge of this wave of life. Someday perhaps I will tell them stories about their grandfather and times long ago, and one afternoon spent sitting on a rock, chasing dinosaur tracks, and marveling at the wonder of it all.

Pots of Cream

Pots and jars and bottles and every sort of container and canister. Curling irons, hair dryers, tools for applying mascara, and a thing for curling eyelashes that looks as though it's a cast-off torture device used in the Spanish Inquisition to pluck out eyeballs.

They are spread all over our house, in the bathrooms, in the kitchen, next to my wife's bedside table, taking up an enormous amount of space, far more than her fair share, and leaving oily little footprints where they have been sitting too long. There are parts of the house where I dare not turn around too suddenly, for fear that I will upset and spill ten or twenty bottles of unidentified "stuff," thereby wasting two hundred dollars of precious extracts, essences, and emollients. Or possibly creating an as-of-yet undiscovered toxic brew, which will eat its way through to the center of the Earth, destroying the orbital stability of the planet, causing it to fly off into interstellar space.

I once took an inventory, making a count of the total number of items she has—including all the makeup stuff and the tools used for applying, smoothing, curling, and refinishing. I lost count three times, and finally gave up at eighty-seven distinct bottles, jars, and tubes of stuff, plus assorted gadgets. I do not understand why she needs so much of it. And for the life of me, I can't get any idea of what they all are for. Just looking at the names confuses me. Men's stuff is straightforward. If it's shaving cream, it says so in large bold letters on the can, in plain English, **SHAVE CREAM**. Pumice soap is simply SOAP. But my wife's bath stuff has curious names like *Sea Salt Stress Bath, Extremely Efficient Emergency Cleansing Mask,* and *Tea Tree Root Exfoliating Foot Bath.*

I started out trying to decipher the uses for these brews, based upon their labels. The last one, for example, I'd guess is made of Tea Tree root. Now I thought tea grew on bushes, but let's assume there is a tea tree out there somewhere. And it must be for exfoliation, the removal of the outer layers of skin, from her feet, presumably by soaking them in the stuff. Why not just use a pumice stone? Wouldn't that be just as effective? Or for that matter, if it's a real problem, I keep a bench grinder in the garage. And it's double insulated, so it's probably safe to use in the bathroom.

Marie owns about a dozen potions that seem to be solely for the removal of that dead skin. Women must generate a great amount of dead tissue but are unable to get rid of it easily. I imagine that my wife's ancestors must have rubbed themselves against rocks and trees to get rid of all their dead skin. In addition to the exfoliation stuff, she has another dozen jars full of stuff for the removal of oils from the skin. Then she has about fifteen bottles of goo for the replenishment of the natural oils of her skin, the oils that she had just removed with the stuff in the oil removal jars.

It strikes me as odd that she would need more than one jar of each general type of stuff. But I have been informed that each one is for a different part of the body. You can't use the same sandpaper to put a rough finish on fir that you use to get a fine surface on oak. I guess I can understand that. So some of the goop is for the elbows. Some of it is for the feet, some for the skin around the eyes, still more for the forehead, the calves, the elbows, etcetera.

But I don't understand why she needs to zap all the oil from her body if she is just going to turn around and put a synthetic replacement in its place. There's some explanation, like cleaning off the oil and the dirt, exfoliating the outer layers of skin, and replenishing with a healthy, natural oil, to keep the skin supple and wrinkle free. Couldn't you just sponge off the excess oil from the greasy parts and reapply it to the dry parts? That'd be pretty natural.

In addition to all the goop and glop she spreads on herself, my wife has a collection of power and hand tools that she uses to compose her outside appearance every morning. I am sure that if the high-pitched buzz of the hair dryer doesn't ruin her hearing, she will electrocute herself with the curling iron.

I have to give her credit. The stuff she buys falls into the category of green and cruelty-free—no animal testing, recyclable or refillable containers, and most are made from natural raw materials. I sometimes think that this is the modernized version of the medicine man or tribal healer, using the bounty of flowers and plants to produce healthy and beneficial remedies for what ails a body. And her collection of pots keeps growing.

The other day, I noted that in addition to all the bits of loofa, natural sponges, and the collected bathing, cleansing and hair-care products she has in the shower, a pair of yellow latex gloves with deep red stains had appeared. And the shower drain had plugged up, was slow to drain, as if blocked by some object or objects. With a long history of my wife and beauty products under my belt, I did not jump to the obvious conclusion that she had brutally murdered someone in our bath.

Though, for a moment, I considered what I might find when I ran the snake down into the drain, and I decided that liquid drain opener might be the wiser move.

In truth, she wears the gloves when she washes her hair, to apply a conditioner that enhances the natural red in her hair. At first I accused her of dying her hair, which she emphatically denied. To prove her wrong, I applied a heaping handful to my own scalp, to my mousy brown hair. I sang a little rub-it-in-your-face kind of song, as I swirled and massaged the goop into my roots and hair. La-li-la-li-la, I'm right and you're wrong, la-li-la-li-la.

Stepping out of the shower, I pointed at my head and said "Ha! It is a dye, isn't it!" in my best Perry Mason voice. I stood there, bare-butted, dripping water all over the floor, with a wide, triumphant smile across my face. My wife looked up for a moment, decided I was having a spell, and went back to brushing her teeth with a look that suggested that she was resigned to being married to me, even if she didn't enjoy it all the time.

Not getting the response I expected, I stomped over to the

mirror and, wiping the steam off the glass, stared at the streaky reflection. Brown hair. Mousy brown, un-red, plain ordinary hair, not a trace of color beyond the norm. But the tips of my fingers, now they were a different story—they were a lovely shade of red that took me three days of soaping, scrubbing, and washing to remove. She told me if I used a loofa, I'd get better results, but I stuck with my Lava soap.

I haven't given her any more grief about that but still suspect that I missed some all important step in the process, like a special catalyst. Or maybe it's just that it doesn't react with your hair unless you're a woman—perhaps it is an estrogen-triggered product.

I have never actually asked her why. As in why she spends so much time applying and spreading and massaging these products into her hair and skin. I have always assumed that she is concerned about aging, about wrinkling, and that by circling the wagons of potted concoctions, perhaps she is doing just that, keeping her skin soft and young. I like her skin a lot, don't see anything wrong with it, and I especially like the person who lives inside it.

I can't help but wonder if any of the myriad collection actually works. It seems to me that if there was one product out there, or maybe two, that actually cleaned, smoothed, and made supple the skin of any woman over the age of twenty-five, we'd know about it. And the person who developed this wonderful material would have retired years ago, after purchasing the entire Hawaiian archipelago with the profits.

Which leads me to one of two possible conclusions. Either the pots and jars and goop don't do anything. Or there is a JFK assassination–sized conspiracy in progress, and the wonder goop is being suppressed by the world's cosmetic and skin-care industries.

My own collection of bath goods and the like is fairly limited. Some shaving soap, shampoo, a bar of soap, and some smelly stuff my children gave me to splash on when I get done shaving. A pitiful collection, when stacked up against my wife's.

Every now and then, I wonder about this. I stand before the bathroom counter and lean real close to the mirror, examining my face carefully. There are a few more lines now, some of which are there only when I smile. I wonder what they will look like in ten or twenty years; a small part of me does not care to find out. There is always a jar of Marie's skin goop nearby. It would be so easy just to spread a little on. But as I consider it, I imagine this going from a small dab at the crow's feet by my eyes to a full-scale smoothing and scrubbing and exfoliating, every day, for the rest of my life.

So I smile once more, and I think how distinguished I will look when the lines really come in.

Birth

S he was born just before nine, Sunday night, to the ringing of
the telephone in our hospital room. My mother, calling long
distance from a trip to California, just in time to hear the opening cries and squalling of her first grandchild.

"Is she born yet?"

I was breathless with fatigue and excitement but managed to
burst out laughing and crying all at once. "Do you hear her?
That's Sarah. Sarah Gwyneth. You're a grandmother!"

I juggled the phone, trying to hold it against my ear with my
shoulder while the doctor told me how to cut the umbilical
cord, and not to hand him back the scissors when I finished. Utterly wiped out by the emotional high, I was more than a little
dumbstruck by the fact that I was really and truly a father.
Somewhere in our collection of baby photos, there is a shot of
me sitting and holding Sarah, leaning on the elbow of my free
arm. And any time I look at that picture, I can conjure up that

feeling—the stunned sense that I am responsible for the life of another human being. My little girl. Sarah Gwyneth Fulghum, my first child, a redhead with blue eyes and porcelain skin, her mother's daughter in looks, but my child in temperament.

Sarah's birth was a moment of such joy and relief. It had been a long day, the labor lasted twenty hours, and Marie was exhausted from the effort and the pain of the contractions, as well as the delivery itself. Now she cried helplessly, cooing "Hello, Sarah" as her baby, all pink and squashed looking, snuggled up to her breast.

The day before, around noon, I had been on the roof cleaning the outsides of the second-floor windows. Marie waddled into the room and opened the window I was working on, a wide smile gracing her face. "Soon," she had said. "It will be very soon."

This is not the sort of news that is either wise or safe to tell a fellow when he's fifteen feet up over a concrete walkway. I dug into my work with renewed spirit, finishing the windows and the rest of my Saturday chores, anticipating. The day flew by and nothing happened. That evening, I worked late, writing a report that was due Monday, making sure that I had it out of the way. I was restless, but I finally drifted off just before midnight, gently rubbing Marie's neck, thinking about what was about to happen. And about twenty minutes later, Marie woke me, telling me NOW it really was time, LET'S GO!

I grabbed the baby bag, which had been packed and ready for at least two weeks, and helped Marie get dressed and ready. We made it to the hospital in just a few minutes, and I had an immediate moment of panic when there was no one manning the check-in desk. In the excitement, I forgot all of the instructions that we had been given, about how and where to check in, where to go, and what to do. We were ushered in and out of rooms, signed papers, and the whole time I wondered which was more important, the baby or the forms. I had a second moment of panic when it occurred to me that if the baby came before we finished all the papers, they might refuse to do anything about it.

Of course, we managed to survive the red tape, and in due course we saw a doctor. The contractions began to subside after a bit, but the doctor decided that today was going to be the day, so we were checked into a small birthing room on the maternity floor. For the first few hours, we wandered around the hospital ward, getting in our road work, hoping gravity would help move Sarah into launch mode just a little faster. Every so often, we had to stop so Marie could ride out a contraction, breathing and groaning. At those times, I rubbed her back and whispered that it was okay.

Part of our path took us through an intensive care area, occupied mostly by people in the process of dying. Looking in through their doors, I watched some of them, attached to ventilators and cardiac monitors, riding out their last hours on earth. And in spite of my absolutely practical views of such things, I wondered about the relationship between their deaths and my child's birth. If I had believed in reincarnation, I'd have to consider which of the souls leaving from those rooms might wander over to the other side of the building, to become my child. If that could happen, could physical proximity be important to which soul went where?

Watching a birth, especially of your own child, is not like anything you can imagine. During our childbirth class, Marie and I had watched videos of birth, particularly of all the different ways that the mother could deliver—squatting, reclining, on her side. It was a bit like watching an instructional video on how to improve your golf game or tie flies. The voice-over was very clinical, never betraying any common feeling for the sense of wonder that the birth inspired for me.

The reality of birth is stark. Lying there, connected to monitors and IV drips, half naked, is the woman you love, breathing off the pain as an eight-pound bowling ball tries to drop through her pelvis, squeezing her innards out of the way. And any number of nurses and doctors and specialists cruise through every few minutes, checking pulse and blood pressure, examining her cervix to see how open it is. They are shooting for the magic number of 10 centimeters (which all the medical profession now pronounces as "sont-i-meters"). And I wonder how anything the size of a baby can pass safely through a passage four inches across. It is all quite amazing.

And finally the baby's head will appear, looking a lot like a hand grenade, and accompanied by blood and fluids and all sorts of other gook, which will certainly prepare you for changing diapers. The moment of birth is as close as I have ever come to that wonderful release of a childhood Christmas morning, when after an eternity of patience and waiting, you *finally* get to open your gifts.

When our number two child, Max, decided that it was time to make his grand entrance, we were almost lackadaisical in our reaction. We had been watching *Tampopo,* a Japanese movie, and based on our last delivery, we sat down to finish the film, breathing together through the contractions until the movie finished and my in-laws arrived to watch over Sarah. We even rewound the tape, and returned it to the rental shop's drop box, so as not to get a late charge, then stopped to get a latte (decaf, of course) before we headed for the hospital.

The classic image of new fatherhood is of the jittery Dad-to-be pacing the waiting room, chain-smoking, while Mother screams and pushes and sweats in a sterile operating room. This is the way that my generation was born. My father was not present at my birth. In fact, he wasn't even given the option.

I cannot imagine being barred from the delivery room. I cannot imagine being kept away from my wife in this time of joy, or relying on strangers to comfort her through the pain. Secretly, I am grateful that my sex has been spared the experience of childbirth, even though I am jealous as all get out that I will never know what it was like to carry a baby, to feed and nurture it as a part of your body, the way Marie has. It does seem to engender a special bond between them.

An old fellow I used to work for asked me if I had been in the room during the birth, and I said with a smile of course I had. Where else would I have been? He shook his head and told me that I was a braver man than he. He couldn't have handled watching his wife suffer the way she did. I can relate—there *were* times during the delivery that I thought Marie wouldn't be able to take another moment. She was exhausted, and in pain. And somehow, she buckled down and found the strength to keep going.

Marie was once told that after the birth, you forget all of the pain. It was described to her as some sort of magic that the body works on your memory. Marie, always pragmatic, will smile when she tells this story, and pause a moment to let the listener imagine this other wonder of childbirth.

"Of course," she says, "that is malarkey. It hurt like hell, and I remember every last minute of it. But," she continues, hugging whichever child is handy, "it was worth it."

Poker Night

I love my wife, dearly and passionately. She is the brightest star in my sky, and I suspect that she and I will be together until one or the other of us keels over dead, hopefully not any time in the next fifty years. I'd like to say that she is my be-all and end-all, but that wouldn't be true.

You see, there are these moments in my life when I feel anxious, when I have an itch that I just need to get scratched. I recognize that even in the most sensitive husband, there are needs that a wife cannot address or fulfill. This is not a reflection upon the quality of my mate; no slight of her beauty, character, or intellect. There are just some things she cannot and should not do, and in response to these faint ticklings of desire, I must look outside of our marriage to satisfy the longings.

Perhaps you think I speak of matters of physical pleasure, of having a mistress, or dalliances with nameless women in grungy hotel rooms. But regardless of what you might think, I am talking about something deeper, more meaningful, more complex.

No, this is the need for a two pair, a straight flush, three of a kind. The clack of Bakelite chips being tossed into the middle of the table as everyone antes up. The riffling sound that the cards make as they are shuffled. Poker.

Poker is the cause of the slight void in my contentedness; it is the little beastie that rolls around in my brain, clawing at my comfort and complacency until I can't stand it anymore. I feel a hunger for it, an absolute need to get out of the house.

No small children asking if I can help them get the cat out of the refrigerator, no telephone solicitors requesting that I buy whatever trash they want to sell me. A tall cool bottle of beer at my elbow, a cigar smoldering in the ashtray, and a full boat, aces over tens, clutched in the left hand. I love a good poker game, even though I am a mediocre player on my best night. But gambling and profit are not the motive. If I come home with more money than I left with, it is the luck bestowed upon the simpleminded, or perhaps that my partners for the evening happen to be even worse players than I.

To truly satiate the hunger, poker must be played with friends, with buddies, guys you trust. My collection of poker buddies is a comfortable one. I have known one or two of the gang for well over fifteen years, going back to high school. The rest are more recent friends, but no less dear to me. Gathering together is a flashback in a way, putting aside careers and marriages and children long enough to get into the game. There are no excesses—no one drinks heavily, no one gambles too hard, no one overindulges in any part of the evening other than dipping heavily into the taco chips and the moments of good fellowship.

Winning is not the purpose of the evening's entertainment. The reason is to return to running with the wolf pack of little boys that we all once were, to laugh and belch and break wind and not give two cents for anything beyond the moment at hand. It is time to catch up on life over the green felt of the table, tell stories, swap lies, relax.

Bottom line, poker night is the last sacred vestige of sexism, the last bastion in which a group of males can gather, to scratch under their arms, tell jokes in questionable taste, and just have a good time. I know how unenlightened this sounds, but an evening strictly in the company of other men serves some primal need, like gathering around the campfire to tell stories and lies about hunting cave bear and saber-toothed tigers. Underneath everything else, poker is just a simple part of the male ritual. It is a need as basic as leaving the seat of the toilet up. Our nature demands that we do so, our spouses demand that we do not, and in the name of domestic harmony, we comply with her wishes. But when we gather to play poker, the seat is never down.

Poker night is one part of the general collection of things that men feel is distinctly their own. Whether the perception is right or not is unimportant. For example, we tend to sneer at women whom we meet in hardware stores. They are not welcome in lumber, they should not intrude into the power tool section. These are our places, and we choose to protect them from the female influence. Similarly, the male browsing the lingerie section will be targeted by women as a pervert or weirdo.

This is a hold-over from the days of the exclusive Men's Club, when we could legally and ethically practice sexism, standing around in large rooms with mahogany and cherry wood paneling, smoking cigars and drinking brandy from a fine crystal snifter.

The evening out with the boys, playing poker, sounds a little suspect, I admit. But I wonder if that little bit of time away from each other isn't a healthy experience for both husband and wife. My wife occasionally disappears from the house with one of her friends, or her mother, usually to go shopping. She has two or three very close friends, and every now and then they go out for the evening—I suspect that they go to a male strip joint and throw their underwear at the boys as they prance about in intsy-wentsy gold lamé athletic supporters. My wife insists that the evenings are just a chance to have dinner and catch up on life. Either way, it's okay with me. She is entitled to her things, to do what she wants to do to decompress from being around me. I would not intrude on that time, just as she respects the importance of my playing poker.

The poker game is distinctly a man's event, not too distant from a Saturday afternoon at a muddy field in the park, playing "touch" football, where the touch gets a little rough. I know very few women who would play that game, although I do know one or two, and they are good players. Which is probably why we don't invite them to join us.

The Men's Movement

I know this man, early forties. Very bright fellow, a man of re-markable skill and far-ranging imagination. I admire his wit and intelligence, and I have numbered him as one of my best friends for quite a few years. Even though he is ten years my se-nior, I have always thought of him as a peer. His character has always been young and easy, and he is full of a brashness and self-confidence. But trouble has arrived in his life, although I am not sure where it came from, or exactly what it might be. It seems lately that he feels he is suffering from a sense that he is not whole, that some part of his soul has been lost. Apparently he has misplaced it somewhere and cannot remember where he was when he last had it. I'd suggest that he try his other coat, but I have the feeling that he wouldn't see the humor in that.

I sympathize with him. It is troubling when you feel as though you are adrift. I've been there often enough myself. It means being taken over by a very lonely and somber mood. I can't speak for everyone, but I just point the nose into the wind, batten down the hatches, and ride the thing out, figuring that the storm will pass eventually. That's what works for me. But I am mightily confounded by my friend's response. His mood has deepened into something truly black and frightening, and he has felt the need to rip and shred his entire existence to find comfort and safety.

And, for reasons I do not understand at all, he seems to think that he needs to become a Native American—what we used to call Indians, as in Cowboys and Indians.

My friend has joined, bonded with, or epoxied himself to the Men's Movement. On weekends, when we used to enjoy my version of male bonding (watching football and playing with power tools), he now spends his time in the woods, chest bared to the elements, beating a cow-hide drum that he stretched the head of himself (regardless of how the cow felt about that), sitting in sweat lodges with those wiser than he, gaining insight. He says that he is searching for his lost warrior tradition, and grieving for his relationship with his father, apparently an unhappy one. He engages in vision quests, seeking wisdom in messages planted in his brain by spirits or his own subconscious, or something like that. It is all very mystical, he explains with a dreamy, faraway look in his eyes. He never offers explanations of any depth, as though he feels I would not understand, being one of the uninitiated.

He's right, I don't understand. I haven't read the right books, and I have never bothered to spend a weekend sweating for visions. I've sweated over a lot of other things—tests, bills, weddings, and births—but I guess they don't count. So I admit to a great deal of ignorance, but I believe that I am absolutely correct when I say no matter what I do not know about his beliefs, I do know that he is missing at least three points of fact:

One, he isn't a Native American, not by a long shot.
Two, his warrior tradition isn't quite what he would believe it to be.
Three, he probably looks really stupid running around in the woods without a shirt on.

Of course, if he runs around in the woods and hangs out in the sweat-lodge enough, he will probably be able to improve on this last one. But I don't believe that he can do a thing about the Native American part. And I'd guess that in recent centuries, his true, historically accurate warrior tradition has little to do with stalking wild buffalo or members of the Seventh Cavalry. Regardless of that, I have a great deal of sympathy with the idea of men trying to get to know themselves better. I applaud any effort they might make in having better relationships with their father, or anyone else for that matter. But when they get to the Native American part, I have to pull up short and think a bit.

We're talking about a buncha middle-class guys, mostly white Anglo-Saxon, Northern European Protestants whose ancestors applauded or participated in the near genocide of the Native Americans, from smallpox, massacre, and starvation. The same ancestors who eventually parked said Native Americans on reservations thought by most white folk to be godforsaken waste lands. Native Americans can recite a lengthy list of attacks on their cultures, their beliefs, their livelihoods. And now, as the modern white male feels he has lost his warrior tradition, he pretends to become a Native American. Maybe I'm just missing a step in here somewhere, but it just doesn't feel right.

I could talk about the decimation of a people and their culture, and the indecency of latching on to a system of beliefs that were formed over generations and are rooted in a common history and experience that has little to do with the past history of white European males. A warrior tradition, much less cultural tradition, of any kind is a long-term process, rooted in upbringing, daily life, and the sense it derives from the community that owns it. You don't get that by glomming onto someone else's ideas for a weekend or two. No, if the goal of the Men's Movement is to reconnect the Lost Soul of the male with its roots, I would like to suggest that perhaps these guys need to reexamine what their roots are, and think about what their lost warrior tradition is really all about.

My forefathers (if you go back a piece) were Picts, Celts, Britons, Welsh, Angles, Swiss, and Saxons. They were bad-ass mother-jumpers, warriors of the most blood-thirsty type, prone to cutting off their enemies' heads and displaying them when company came over. The fact is some of my kin fought buck-naked except for a coat of blue paint and scared the legions of the Roman Empire so much they built a wall to keep them on the other side—apparently my ancestors were not only unfit for civilized society, they were too much trouble to even try to conquer and grind into submission. My distant ancestors started out as nomadic types, wandering around Northern Europe, fighting, burning, pillaging, pushing other people around, generally causing grief for the neighbors. They were the bad boys of their day. That seems pretty warriorlike to me, and it seems a fairly reasonable warrior tradition to grab a hold of, if you feel the need.

I don't know if my ancestors communed with nature and the Great Spirit in something resembling sweat lodges, or had vision quests, but they spent a lot of time moving big rocks around so they could build things like Stonehenge and Carnac and a lot of other pretty strange and mysterious places, so they must have had some idea about the mystical nature of the universe. In later years, they invented churches with hard pews to sit upon and feel bad about a lot of things they secretly enjoyed doing. That certainly sounds like it must have been a surreal experience, certainly enough to induce some real wisdom.

I don't know if father and son had a better relationship back then. Considering the conditions in ancient Britain, it can't have been improved by the need to struggle and scrabble an existence out of a the big bad world while completely at the mercy of the vagaries of nature. Somehow I think everyone was too busy keeping warm and alive to worry about interpersonal relationships.

If the Men's Movement really wants men to connect with their warrior spirits, then maybe they ought to try this. Go to the hardware store and buy a gallon of water-soluble latex paint in a deep midnight blue and a paint roller. Go out into the woods, strip down to your skivvies, and give yourself two coats. And if you really want to feel primitive, skip the primer. If you aren't of the right heritage to claim this warrior tradition, I'll let you borrow my share on Tuesday nights. I'll be playing poker.

Sarah and Bill

The senior child in our outfit, Sarah, has a thing for Bill Clinton. Now I know that all sorts of allegations have been made about Mr. Bill and philandering, but I don't worry too much about it getting out of hand, since Sarah is now eight and he is fortyish. Still, I keep an eye peeled for love letters doused in Tinkerbell perfume going out in our mail, just in case.

In truth, Sarah's love for the President is of the sort that she reserves for wise and thoughtful leaders, an affectionate loyalty. More of the fairy-tale view of politics; somewhat naive, but entirely reasonable and understandable for a small child—and a point of view not alien to many adults.

Up until October of 1992, Sarah was the staunchest of Republicans. She felt very strongly that we should vote for George Bush because he was the leader, and one should always support the leader. This has to do with a small child's view of good kings and queens. She chastised me very harshly because I supported the Clinton campaign.

She asked me why I would vote for Bill, and how could I be so mean to George Bush. I tried to explain my concerns about the economy, and the overall health of the United States, and most important, I tried to get her to understand that we all have a choice and that I was entitled to mine. Besides, I explained, I get to vote and she doesn't, so there.

These were difficult concepts for Sarah, considering that she was only five years old at the time. And it was patently unfair that she didn't get a voice in the decision.

But then, through some strange twist in her thinking, she decided that she did like Bill Clinton—a lot. I asked her why she had turned on Bush. She said that she heard that George Bush had started a war and people were hurt and killed. She wanted to know if anybody she knew had been hurt and would she and I and her brother and mother get hurt or killed. I tried to explain that, yes indeed, there had been a war, people had been hurt and killed, and that sometimes these things happen when countries can't agree. Unfortunately, her idea that two countries having a fight be relegated to "time-out," while an excellent idea, is not the way these things are commonly handled. Sarah wasn't too happy about that, and she decided that maybe George Bush didn't deserve to be leader anymore.

Of course, 1992's was a three-way election, so next Sarah had to choose between Bill and Mr. Perot. Sarah decided that she didn't like Mr. Perot at all, because he had called Clinton a "chicken-head" during the campaign and that wasn't nice, and that the two of them should be separated until Mr. Perot apologized. I don't recall Perot making that particular statement, but that is what Sarah believed. Sarah decided that we should all vote for Bill.

I took Sarah with me to vote at our local school. She kept looking around at all the faces in the crowd, which was very large. After a bit, she asked me where they were. I asked who "they" were, and she said "George and Bill and Mr. Perot, of course, you silly." Sarah's expectation was that this group of three hundred or so voters was all there was, and that the candidates should be there to smile and shake hands and tell us why we should vote for them. I also think that she wanted to explain to Perot why we don't call names.

Since the election, Sarah has asked several times if she could send drawings she has made to Bill, Hillary, and Chelsea. One of them, a picture of the first family on the White House lawn, was particularly special to her. I knew that the Clintons were busy people just at the moment, so it was unlikely they would ever see Sarah's drawing. The President was getting some ridiculous amount of mail at that time, maybe 100,000 letters a week. But Sarah was adamant.

As luck would have it, I happen to have a friend in Hot Springs, Arkansas, who is a shirt-tail relation of the Clintons. I called him and told him about Sarah and her fascination with the Clintons. As I had hoped he would, he offered to mail the drawing from Hot Springs, Arkansas, home of the Clintons, if I would send it to him. The word in his clan was that if a letter had a Hot Springs postmark, it actually got read.

Sure enough, Sarah got a small note in response. She was thrilled, even though it wasn't personal. From a small child's perspective, a preprinted note with a signature is a big deal, even if it thanks her for her important political views and input, and invites her to lend her support to the current administration's efforts to reshape America.

Since then, Sarah has followed the activities of the President and his family with something like a religious fervor. She worries about how mean the press are to them, especially what they say about Chelsea. Her perception of the Clintons is of a family of three very real people, rather than the pseudo-celebrities that the media makes them into.

It is my hope that the child's fascination with her leader as a fairy-tale prince will someday become an adult's concern for the way the country is run and the integrity and character of the people who run it. Perhaps not. But maybe even a romantic view of politics is better than no view at all.

The Damp
Feeling About
My Ankles

In case you've never had the pleasure of visiting Seattle, let me give you a few general descriptors that will help you picture my home town: wet, with moments of dank, intervals of dripping, and an afternoon deluge. Saying that it has been raining cats and dogs is an understatement. It feels more like elephants, hippos, bull moose, and blue whales. The rains start in October, and pound more or less steadily away at us through May or June, sometimes even into July. At which point the rain will cease altogether and we will have a three-month drought. After a while, you get used to the fact that your lawn is either a mud hole or a stretch of brown, dead grass intent on becoming a fire trap.

During the dry months of this most recent summer, I often wondered if the rainless days might dry up my well, leaving me without drinking or bathing water. I'm not worried about that now. If the well runs dry, I'll just ladle water out of my basement.

We discovered a damp spot in the basement carpet a few days after New Year's Eve. Nothing too big, just a little dark spot. A mild seepage from under the foundation. It happens when you have a basement. I got out my trusty shop-vac, sucked the spot dry, and went happily to bed, leaving a fan running to speed the evaporation. Next morning, the spot reappeared, and had increased rather alarmingly in size, signaling a dangerous problem that might spread like a malignancy. Ah-ha, I said, as the light bulb goes on. Did I check the sump?

The water level in the sump could only be described as having risen. As in it had risen over its banks, spilling water out over the side to meet the water already forcing its way up through the completely sodden concrete floor. But not to worry, I have a pump and some hose. Well, I have a pump, and I did have some hose. But somehow the hose had sneaked off, either evaporated into the atmosphere or stolen by Gypsies. Or possibly I just can't remember where I put it.

On a panicked trip to the hardware store with two small children in tow, I snapped up two twenty-four-foot lengths of inch-and-a-half drain line, clamps, an extra pump (just in case), and a dozen other small odds and ends I might need. Everything except a hose coupling. Of course, the sump is about thirty feet from the basement sink. I need to connect both hoses together, but I have no coupling. And the water had now ascended to a quarter inch deep.

Being an inventive soul, I took out my trusty hacksaw and applied it to the washing machine hose, sacrificing a ten-dollar drain hose for lack of a fifty-cent coupling. Hoses were spliced, and the pump was primed and dropped into the pit, where it began to whir and whir and *whir,* spitting water out at an alarming rate but definitely lowering the level of the sump. I went to bed, assuming that the basement would be damp but drier by morning, feeling a masculine tool-user's glow of victory at my ability to fix things up. The kind of feeling that Roosevelt must have had when they opened the Panama Canal. Throw me a problem, I am man, I shall prevail.

HA! The decks were awash by morn. The water in the low spot in the center of the room was now an inch deep, and only slightly behind it was the family room and the hallway where the hose lay, spitting little sprinkler jets of mist all over from small, pin-prick–sized holes. It seems that the cat, in a midnight fit of feline jocularity, decided to attack the hose as it thrummed and quivered with its load of water. Perhaps the cat thought it was a thirty-foot-long black boa constrictor. The cat attacked, clawing and kicking and scratching and puncturing. And the pump merrily spat water all over the floor and walls all night, where it could make its way back to the sump, to be sprayed all over my floors and walls in an eight-hour festival of recycled damp.

Not to mention the fact that outside our abode the gutters were overflowing, dumping gallons and gallons of Seattle's "Liquid Sunshine" (if I ever catch the guy who came up with that, I'll drown him in my shop-vac and bury him in my drain field) onto the gravel walkway that surrounds the house, where it could seep down the foundation wall and into—you guessed it—my basement.

As I say, Seattle has this reputation of being gray, rainy, cloudy, and dismal. It is not a completely undeserved reputation, and one assumes that the first settlers could not have arrived here in the fall. I've lived here all my life, and I can say that after a time you get used to the weather, just like you learn to live with snow in Boston and humidity in Houston.

But this last winter, with my basement flooding, it finally got to me. It rubbed me the wrong way, and I briefly contemplated relocating to some place dry and arid. In the meantime, I have decided that I have some sense of how the Captain of the *Titanic* must have felt. Hulled forward, water rising, no land or help in sight. The poor man must have muttered a rather emphatic Damn! to himself. And I could not agree more. But it wasn't a complete loss. I at last understand why basements aren't built in this part of the world anymore.

I briefly toyed with the notion of setting the house on fire, and rebuilding from the ground up—starting by filling in the basement with five hundred tons of waterproof concrete. But when I realized that the water in the basement would no doubt douse the flames, I was so dejected I couldn't even bring myself to wallop the cat.

Heavy with Child

Here I am on the escalator, staring at myself in the mirrors that line every surface. I am decked out in the uniform of the new-born parent: diaper bag on one shoulder, complete with clean and dirty diapers, bottles, extra clothes (size *teeny*), wipes, spit-up rags, tissues, pacifiers, rattles, and assorted toys. All of the items required for the shortest trip with one small child. On the other shoulder, nicely balancing the diaper bag, are two shopping bags so heavy with towels and baby clothes that my fingers are tingling as the loop handles dig into them. Slung in front of me, my son, Max, is asleep in his carrier, periodically kicking me in the bladder as he dreams of who knows what.

We are at the mall, shopping the white sale along with a couple of thousand mothers and small children. We manage to stand out though, because I am not Max's mother but his father. As I pause to catch my breath, people stop and examine Max, then smile at me. "What a cute baby," they say. "How nice of you to let your wife have the day off."

Most people assume that I am baby-sitting when they see me with my kids and without my better half. It is treated as something of a miracle when I change a diaper in public. A clerk at a department store once said it was *nice* that I was taking care of the baby on my lunch break. I informed her that I was the *primary care provider,* a term my wife told me to use. The clerk looked at me as though I had three heads and a tail.

Before Max was born, we assumed that when he arrived my wife would take the usual maternity leave to look after him, as she had done with our first child. And then Max comes along and destroys that vision of domestic bliss with an emotional charge equal to a couple of hundred pounds of high explosive. *Boom.* Max was only hours old when we were informed that he had a heart murmur. A week later a cardiologist said the murmur was caused by a congenital problem called a "ventricular septal defect," or VSD, which simply put is a big hole between the two lower chambers of the heart. Blood that should have been flowing into his aorta was instead flowing back into the vein that came from his lungs. He struggled to breathe and eat, and he was a skinny, haggard baby. If Max did not have open heart surgery to correct the VSD, he would die.

There are moments in life when one is overwhelmed by an emotional wave of such magnitude that all rational control founders. In the instant following the doctor's pronouncement of Max's condition, I found I could not speak, I could not breathe. At that single moment in time, all of the years I had spent developing into an adult were gone, and the confidence I felt as a parent betrayed me by vanishing. I could do nothing but weep. When such moments knocked me flat as a child, I had known a grown-up would be there to make life safe and good once again. As an adult, I realized that *I* was now the grown-up, and no one could make the problem just go away. Time to buckle down and be tough—even though I wanted to run and hide.

We had assumed that Max, like his sister Sarah, would stay home with his mom for eight weeks and then go to daycare. But now Max would not be able to go to daycare until after he had recovered from his surgery. And there was no way of knowing when the surgery might be. We only knew that the older he was when it happened, the better his chances would be. Both of us pondered quitting our jobs, but fortunately my company offered me a working leave. I would be able to stay home and work when I could, and care for Max as long as needed. The eighth Monday of Max's life, I began my turn watching him, to be his "mother" according to Webster's, and to work when I could.

And at age nine and a half weeks, the day of Max's surgery came. We went to the hospital on a Wednesday morning and checked in. We held Max a lot and tried to comfort him, as he wasn't allowed to eat before the surgery. He was kept in a pre-op ward with about eight other children, all of whom were waiting to be called for surgery. We were approached by people doing studies on this and that, and wanting us to allow Max to participate. We met all the doctors and assistants and nurses and the anesthesiologist, and other people I don't recall, and they all told us what would happen. The last person we met was the surgeon, who was a quiet man who looked like he had had better days. Briefly, he told us the same thing everyone else had been telling us all day: Max would be anesthetized before they cut from the bottom of his rib cage to the top, cutting through the ribs and tissue to open him up sort of like those little cereal boxes we used to get in elementary school. They call it "cracking the chest," but the doctors didn't use that expression within our hearing.

They would stop Max's heart and circulate his blood through a heart-lung machine to supply his body with oxygen. Meanwhile, the surgeon would open Max's heart, and sew a Dacron patch over the hole. The amazing thing is that this little bit of Dacron would most likely cure Max's problem for the rest of his life. In fact, with time his body would incorporate the fabric into the heart, covering it with natural tissue. I know I heard all of this at the time because I can recite it here, but then all I wanted was someone to tell me that it was all going to be okay, that my son would be all right.

You know that everyone will die eventually. You may hope for them to go painlessly in their sleep. You rarely think about delivering a loved one up to a doctor for a procedure that may kill them. I could barely consider this, but while I was hoping for the best, I was preparing for the worst.

We spent hours waiting in a lobby outside the surgical wing, sitting in the stink of unwashed bodies with dozens of other people. All of them were hurting, worried about their children. Some of them left in tears as the worst possible thing happened. The day of Max's surgery two children didn't make it. I kept thinking that the high chance that my son would survive was offset by the small chances that some of the other children had. I felt guilty about that for months. The surgeon took my son away, cracked him open, and patched the hole. About a week after that, Max came home.

After the swing of emotions—shock, fear, hope, and relief—the calm of caring for my child was a welcome one. It took me months to realize how tough a job just being a daddy could be.

Full-time parenting is hard work, and I do not believe that the strain of holding a full-time job and being an evening-and-weekend parent really prepares you for the task. We of the two-income-family generation cannot comprehend what many of our stay-at-home mothers did as a matter of course, but I now feel a greater sense of the importance my children have to me, and what it means to be a father—or more important, a parent.

And I learned from the comments of both passing strangers and close friends that the common view is that fathers are not parents.

A woman called our house once to ask my wife to answer a survey about cloth diapers. I told her that since I did half of the diaper changing, I would be glad to talk to her. She balked, and then informed me that the company paying for the survey had specified that only mothers be allowed to respond. I suppose that the survey results wouldn't be as smooth if they said "Three out of five mothers surveyed, and this one father we talked to, prefer cloth diapers."

All of this experience with Max took place almost five years ago. When I got Max up this morning and stripped off his pajamas to get him dressed for school, I looked at the horrible, jagged scar that runs from the top of his ribcage nearly to his belly button, and the little dimple in his belly where a tube drained the blood from his chest cavity. When I look at him this way I sometimes cry, remembering how scared I was, horrified that we might lose our little boy.

This morning, though, I smiled. Because this child, who was

once pale and thin and at times seemed barely alive, has become a solid, tough little fellow. His sister will cry when scolded, but Max will pull in his chin and glare at you. This little boy who jumps and laughs and likes to build things, who chases the cats, and likes to ride in his daddy's truck is alive and full of life in every respect. I sometimes think that because of the surgery Max has unconsciously decided to take life by the throat and live it to its fullest. He has only one speed, and that is full-tilt boogie. He sometimes points to the scars and says, "I gotta scratch, but I'm okay now." Max's scars don't mean fear to me anymore; they mean life!

Barf

I don't care if you live in Cleveland, Nairobi, or Frankfurt, if you have kids, you've been dipped in gooh, those smelly, sticky, nasty green or brown effluents that leak out of little children. Gooh that, given your druthers, you wouldn't touch even if you were wearing a chemical warfare suit. Not just the old standards, like poop, but the truly awful glop.

It is unfortunate that we can't use gooh as an alternative energy source, because little children produce it in prodigious quantity, and there is no good means of disposal. From upper and lower orifices, clasped in their fingers at dinner, out their noses and ears, rivers and lakes and oceans of gooh flow. And someone has to clean it up.

In our family, that someone, as you may have guessed, is me. One of my Dad duties is as the *Official Gooh Catcher and Clean-Up-After-the-Spillage Guy*. I shoulder this duty more or less willingly. My wife is a tough woman, no nonsense about her, but when confronted with a small barf-covered child, she turns green, folds and crumbles, and hands the child to me. I could object, but if I do, I'll then have to clean up two messes— the first one made by the child, and the second one produced by my wife in sympathetic nausea.

I'm not saying that I enjoy this job, but I've been specially trained to ignore gooh, vomit, and other effluents by virtue of serving as attendant during the births of my children. One of the first thing a child does after birth is void all the stuff collected over the previous nine months. Medical science even bestowed a special name on the stuff, calling it meconium—probably ancient Greek for gooh. I don't really know where the name comes from, but it does not do justice to the greenish substance, sort of a textural cross between road tar and guacamole, with the smell of skunk. The stuff is rancid, and your child will offer it up to you, usually in a Kodak moment, as she nuzzles your shoulder, or lies with your wife, nursing. Adding injury to insult, the stuff takes forever to scrub off.

It's a "Hi mom, hi dad. See what I made for you?" kind of moment. It makes you think that if this is the worst clean-up detail you will ever face down, you can handle anything that follows.

The child, however, is only toying with you. There is a temporary lull, as your child nurses on breast milk, and produces diapers filled with a brownish material not unlike applesauce. It doesn't smell too bad, and as you change these diapers, you think that you could handle this. What's all the fuss over smelly diapers? No problem!

And then they start eating real food, like those little jars of smashed green beans, pureed meat substance, and stuff with a hue that advertises itself as fruit of some kind. Your outlook on the world changes radically. All of a sudden, that sweet-smelling baby begins to smell bad—not all the time, mind you, just four to eight times a day. Right as you sit down for a quiet cup of coffee, the child turns red, straining for a moment, gurgles and pops, and produces the unmistakable aroma that lets you know that by the time you get back from the changing table, your coffee will be cold.

If they aren't making dirty diapers for you, then they're on your shoulder, being burped, making gooh at that end. People call it all sorts of nice things, like spitting up. In case you're wondering about the distinction, babies spit up, women vomit, children puke, and men and dogs barf.

I was at a business meeting one day when my children were still in the burping stage. I reached into my overcoat pocket to stash my gloves out of the way, and buried my fingers to the second knuckle in a used spit-up rag. The sensation of sticky, squishy ick caused me to recall that I had been burping my daughter on my shoulder just before I left the house that morning. Upon achieving the desired belch, I handed her back to my wife and, without thinking, shoved the rag into my coat pocket. And there it was, an unofficial reminder (with a slightly curdled smell) of my fatherdom.

But for spitting up, the first three Christmas mornings were the worst. Each year the children whipped themselves into a frenzy of excitement, anticipating the arrival of Santa, and finally getting to open all those presents. Of course, the stockings were filled with candy canes, chocolate, and other assorted sweets. Inevitably the child eats some of this. And usually with the blessing of the parents. "Hey, it's Christmas!" we reasoned, not realizing what the toxic blend of edibles and circumstance has created.

Add sugar to a small child's empty tummy at eight o'clock in the morning, factor in warp speed as the child tears into present after present, joggling and bouncing, growing more and more excited. The stomach begins to churn a little, the tension builds, she adds enough candy to the mixture to achieve critical mass. And then it happens. Within seconds, the child's demeanor changes, she turns to alabaster, her cheeks get cold, and she ceases all activity. The eyes glaze over.

For the new parent, the reaction is to rush up to the child, concerned and worried, to cuddle up close and ask what can be wrong on this most special of mornings. Whereupon the child explodes. *FOOO-Waaaah!* A gusher! And the poor parent is covered in gooh. At this point the child fully recovers, feels fine, and carries on with the demolition of gifts as the foolish adult retires to the bathroom to hose off the urp, washing and re-washing to get rid of *that* smell.

The more experienced parent knows better. When the child's color drops off in the middle of the fun, we hustle the kid down the hall, to be in close proximity to the toilet. And we always stay behind the child.

I won't go into all the other stuff that can flow from a child. You've seen it, you've cleaned it up, and because of this, you and I have the shared experience of gooh that bonds us together. And no doubt you've dealt with cleaning up externally gener-ated gooh, what they call "sensory explorations." This is a nice way of saying that the kid just put both hands into her plate of cooked squash, squished and squeezed it between the fingers for a bit, and then planted the now orange muck right in her hair.

Thank God for soap and water.

But the wonder years pass too quickly. The child learns to walk and talk, blow her nose, and "hold it" until a toilet is available. Before you know it she is operating the VCR and making her own scrambled eggs. Too quickly the baby is gone and in its place there's a functional person. I miss those early years dearly, even if it sometimes meant embracing and comforting a child coated with an indescribable crust of gooh and never saying "Ack."

Do Not Try
This at Home

E very Monday through Friday morning, I pack both children up into the car, and we trundle down the road, destined for school. Some mornings this is easy; they are excited about being there, playing and learning. Mornings when I am going to the airport to leave on a business trip after I drop them at school can be pretty rough. Frequently the question "Why are you going away?" gets asked by a child with her head turned down, a puffy lower lip extending out in a petulant look she has probably practiced in the mirror.

This is my job, I try to tell them. To earn a living, to provide shelter, food, clothing, and Barbie Dolls for my children—these are my duties, and they require that I toil at an occupation. Part of my duties require that I fly to other cities, to work on fixing things there, to meet with my clients. My oldest child understands that I am an engineer, that I do things with electricity, fixing important stuff that helps airplanes land, that help people talk to each other over the phone. She has an inkling of what this means, and with the passing of time, she has become a little more understanding about my work and its demands upon my time. The justification seems to hold water, especially if I bring a gift or three back with me, although she holds my boss personally responsible for my absence and doesn't like him very much.

My son is under no such burden. He knows that I am an engineer, and he does not understand why I have to leave town to drive a train. And not only does he give me grief over this, but he is very distressed that I will not take him for a ride on my train, to let him run the throttle, blow the whistle, and call for more coal to be shoveled into the boiler. That is what engineers do, run locomotives, and good and kind engineers let their little boys ride in the engine, and at least blow the whistle.

Whether or not he ever forgives me for this trespass, I can only wait and see. In the meantime, I tried to make him understand what I really do for a living, that there is a reason that he cannot drive my train. I attempted this by kneeling on a threadbare blue carpet, in front of my son and his class at school. My job for an hour or so was to be the teacher, telling this collection of five-year-old minds all about electricity. I opened with the usual disclaimer—Do not play with electricity without express written permission from your parents, signed and witnessed. After we'd gotten the required warnings and cautions out of the way, we went at the fun big time.

I had a box full of parts and doo-dads and gizmos, handfuls of integrated circuits, diodes, resistors, capacitors and all sorts of bits, for the kids to handle. And a set of battery packs, each wired up with a light bulb so the kids could see what electricity will and will not go through, and they were very excitedly testing everything in the room—chairs, pencils, paper, their shoes, each other, the guinea pig, me. We talked about why electricity goes through things, and what makes electricity, and we did some cheap theatrics, making static electricity and a simple electromagnet. The kids said "Gosh!" and "Wow!" a lot, showing that they were both interested and impressed, but overall I felt that the children were a lot more coherent about electronics than I was at that age. I suppose it comes from living in a world full of cellular phones and VCRs.

The big finale was a plasma globe, a glass ball filled with a rarefied atmosphere of gases; when plugged into a wall outlet, it sent streamers of electricity arcing across the ball. When you touch the surface of the ball, all the electricity comes to your hand or finger or whatever you've touched it with. The children were nervous at first, since they knew that electricity is dangerous, but after the first two or three kids tried it without lighting up, they were inching forward from their seats, anxious to get a turn.

I enjoyed myself so much. Getting to go to school again, and show something that is both practical, educational, and perhaps just a little bit cool. The children were young enough not to worry about right answers. They had an open-eyed enthusiasm for the experience at hand. My son was alive with chat about the "speriments," and I think that I raised his status among his peers by being a dad who can do cool stuff.

When I picked the kids up later that afternoon, I was presented with a huge sheet of paper, thanking me for coming, and telling me what each child liked best, and decorated with pictures of the things we did, and inviting me to come back with more neat stuff. My son talked about that morning for a week afterward.

The best part is that my son now believes that my job has a lot to do with electricity, cool little experiments, electromagnets, doo-dads and gee-gaws that make little children go WOW! If only my real job was even remotely like that.

The reality is that after that demonstration, my child's view of my work is still pretty well off the mark. Yes, I do things that involve electricity, but it is all hypothetical. On a daily basis, my closest contact to electricity is turning my light switch and computer on. Whether they think I am flying off to faraway cities to fix airports, sitting behind the throttle of a 90-ton diesel electric, or that I spend all day messing with electronic toys, neither of my children really has an inkling of what my day is like.

I don't work in a mad scientist's laboratory; there are no crackling power supplies or flashing lights. I spend most days in a relatively small cubicle about nine feet on a side. Most of my space is consumed by paper, piled high with books and reports. When I'm there, if I'm not buried in my in-basket, or sorting through the nit-picking details of a project's design, I am in meetings with clients and other engineers, discussing the merits of this thing and that approach, developing specifications and cost estimates. Some days it becomes painfully dull and only the necessity of doing the job right keeps it interesting. And most important, it is my job.

There are days, arriving early on a sunny spring day, with a really good cup of fresh coffee, when I sit down at my desk and look east. Off that way, out the window on the other side of the hall, I can see the peaks of the Cascade Mountains, fifty or so miles away. Whether they are trimmed with snow, or showing the green of the forests, they always look inviting.

After a moment, I turn my back to the window, so as not to be completely unproductive, and I try to focus on the stacks of drawings and blueprints in front of me.

Then there's a thought in the back of my brain, that up in those mountains there is a railroad track, running high above the rivers, cutting through the flanks of the mountains in long tunnels. And I think about the real engineer up there, watching the forests and hills rolling by, as his train rumbles across trestles and bridges.

Fulghumbia

In the past few years I have noticed that we've done a lot of incorporating around my hometown. Former burgs are now the cities of Seatac and Woodinville. On an international scale, it has become in vogue for the country wishing to be considered hip to secede from whatever union it used to belong to and form a new nation state. The nations formerly known as Czechoslovakia, the Soviet Union, and the mess that once was Yugoslavia are all giving it a shot—not always with great success. But at least the makers of flags and atlases must be very happy, not to mention the professional composers of national anthems.

At first, this all seems rather silly. What ever happened to the idea of a united world, of a global community? Why create even more borders to cross or defend, more levels of taxation and bureaucracy? Then again, if you consider the benefits, maybe it's not such a bad idea after all.

So I would like to announce that I have decided, due to economic, political, cultural, and religious reasons, to declare myself, my family, and my home as a separate and sovereign nation, the Independent Federated State of Fulghumbia, population 4.

We are very proud of our country. We have a full employment economy, no crime of any sort (other than cheating on the *New York Times* crossword), no pollution to speak of, no racial unrest, and peaceful relations with the neighbors. We have the lowest tax rate possible (0.0 percent), and a reasonably high per capita income. Our work force is well-trained in technical and business practices, and we welcome foreign investment.

We are a peaceful people. To date, there have been no wars involving our nation, and our national defense budget is zero. And we are a nuclear-free zone. Given the opportunity, we will happily sign the nuclear nonproliferation treaty.

To support the drive toward continuing democracy in our nation, we will be asking for a modest amount of foreign aid, say $200,000 a year, from the United States of America, in exchange for which we will grant fishing rights and access to our ports by U.S. ships (if we can ever afford some waterfront or a pool), and we will allow over-flights of our territory by U.S. commercial and military aircraft. I expect that the State Department will be glad to grant such a modest request in the light of the billions that they are spending on less friendly and cooperative governments.

In support of good trade relations with the U.S., we will agree to purchase 95 percent of our goods from American retailers. Of course, as foreigners, we will not pay taxes, and we shop duty-free every time we drive home from work.

Borders are no problem. To exit or enter Fulghumbia, we do not require a passport or visa, just a valid driver's license. As of this writing, no border checkpoints have been established and we have had no problems with illegal immigration. We do not, however, allow door-to door-solicitation. If you come by trying to sell anything other than Girl Scout Chocolate Mint cookies, we shall have no choice but to politely decline. Unless, of course, you persist, in which case the head of Internal Security will give you a dressing-down. He may even be rude.

As you might expect, there are a few downsides and problems associated with our fledgling nation. It is impractical for us to send a delegation to the United Nations, and we are only able to field embassies when we travel abroad. I would be remiss in not admitting that we have been forced to double, triple, and even quadruple up our assignments, due to our limited population (four). I am President, Speaker of the Parliament, Mayor of the capital city, and Ministers of Information, Public Works, and Transportation. My wife has been elected Leader of the Loyal Opposition, Member of Parliament, Ministers of Finance, Foreign Affairs, and Tourism. The remaining members of our populace are too young to be elected yet, although a referendum is on the floor of the Parliament for lowering the voting age to five.

I will close by including a pitch from the Ministry of Tourism. Fulghumbia welcomes you. We have world-class facilities, including hot and cold running water that is completely safe to drink, electric lights, and an excellent native cuisine. English is the national language (although we can oblige you with a bit of Spanish, French, and Swahili), and there are no problems with electricity for those of you from North America.

We use 120 Volt 60 cycle just like you. If you are interested in the great outdoors and scenic beauty, we have plentiful trees, a rolling lawn, and hiking suited for even those of the most feeble constitution. Stop by for the Annual Full-Contact Lawn Bowling and Croquet Tournament, held every May. We look forward to the day when the sport catches on and our national team can march proudly into the Olympic Stadium under the great banner of Fulghumbia.

X
Chromosome

As a rule, children are socialists.

They believe that they are equal, that everything must be fair, especially when they are on the short end of the stick. My own children certainly subscribe to this view. Life should be, nay, *must* be fair. Never mind that they are two and a half years apart at ages where that matters (eight and five). If one child gets something or some privilege that is of given size and value, the other child must have the same. For example, if Sarah is allowed to select a bit of candy at the store, say a Hershey bar with almonds, Max will not select, under any circumstances, an item of candy which has a lower value or size. He will not pick a piece of penny candy because it is one-fifth the size of the chocolate bar his sister is getting—unless he can pick out five pieces of penny candy, to create the right balance. Max would not object to taking ten pieces, if he could get away with it, but he instinctively understands that this would violate the rules of equality. I believe that in military circles this is known as the balance of power.

My children the socialists believe in equality and fair play, but I am a realist, well aware of the fact that life is not fair. It is not fair that I am too short and too clumsy to play professional basketball for wonderfully obscene amounts of money. It is, however, the way life is, and I feel no need to sue the NBA or my pediatrician over the inequity. It is something I have learned to live with.

Regardless of what the children think, they may be equal but they are not the same. The difference in their ages matters. Their abilities to do things and take responsibility is different. And finally, there is a distinct difference, a unique character to each child, that I can only attribute to their genders.

To illustrate: Sarah flashes past, a shock of red hair with a streak of pink hair ribbons trailing behind; then, just as quickly as she burst into my field of vision, she has turned a one-eighty and is headed back to her room. Her pink room, with its pink carpet, pink walls, frilly curtains, and a mountain of stuffed animals sitting at one neatly made end of her bed. Moments later, she is kneeling on the floor, rummaging around in her collection of stuff for the right purse, and the right stuff to fill it. With the right stuff in hand, she is up, and headed for the front door. But as she slams the door open, it occurs to her that she doesn't have the right shoes. And another trip is made, back to her room to find just the right pair. In the end, she decides on the white high-tops with the sparkly pink laces. They go best, she says, with her outfit—a dress covered with six-inch sunflowers, a black hat, and pink tights. Personally, I think that the black high tops with the plain white laces were fine. But I am a father, and as a male, I do not understand what it means to accessorize properly.

I am well aware that by the time I see her at the end of the day, she will have changed, at least once, using the copious supply of extra outfits she carries in her bag. It is always a little confusing to arrive to pick her up, looking for a little girl in a dress, only to discover her careening around the monkey bars in shorts and a T-shirt.

Max trundles past, with his coat and lunchbox. Semiclean blue jeans, beat up tenny runners, and a faded T-shirt are his choice for the day. He would select the same clothes every day, given the opportunity. He has asked frequently if he can't wear his pajamas to school, to save time; besides, he likes his pajamas. I object on the sole basis that frequently his pajamas consist of an oversized T-shirt and a pair of Batman underpants. Hardly appropriate attire for the learning experience.

His hair is a cross between Alfalfa's bowl cut and the professional athlete's shaved look. (I keep asking his mother to inscribe his name in the back, or color it orange like Dennis Rodman, but she declines to accept my suggestions). He is reasonably clean this morning, although since he will spend the day digging holes to find buried treasure or trap squirrels in, he will be filthy by the time I collect him in the afternoon, dirt ground into the knees of his pants, and his shoes and pockets filled with sand and small rocks. At least he will be wearing the same clothes that I delivered him in.

Sarah lives in her ocean of pink, but Max's room is the utilitarian-male space. His room, done up with dark carpeting, and pine furniture, is a jumble of Tinker Toys and wooden blocks, with dirty clothes put everywhere except in the hamper.

The Legos are built into castles and machines, space ships, and fighter jets. In one corner sits one of Max's favorite toys, a big box full of wood scraps with a small hammer, a measuring tape, a carpenter's apron, and a jar of nails.

Max lives in a sea of clutter and confusion, but Sarah stacks, sorts, inventories, and organizes her stuff, putting the mountain of stuffed animals just so on the end of her bed (they are arranged according to a complex plan accounting for size, shape, and seniority). Chief overlord of them all is a beautiful porcelain doll that she got from Ed and Marie, neighbors of her grandparents. She plays with it with a gentle reverence, understanding what a fine and beautiful thing it is. So far, she has kept it intact—largely because her brother cannot reach it.

The two children are often to be found outside, playing some complicated game together. The theme and nature of the game depends on who got to decide. When Sarah chooses the game, it is a passionate drama of love, relationships, and the like, with at least one princess and prince and a witch or two. For Max, it is soldiers, or pirates crossing the seas in their frigate, looking for unwary Spanish treasure galleons to sink. Max will quite willingly play the games his sister suggests, but they are not the sorts of things he would come up with on his own. And the same is true of his sister. She will pretend to hobble with a pirate peg leg and slash at imaginary enemies with a pretend sword, but she will do it with considerably less enthusiasm than Max might like.

Sarah is older and more reliable, and I trust her to use my computer unattended. In a pinch, she will come find me and ask for help. Max, by contrast, would take a screwdriver to the hard drive and CPU in a fit of small male tool-making-and-problem-solving, and present me with his solution—"Daddy, the computer didn't work, so I took the parts out and *washed* them for you. They were very dirty."

The differences are pretty clear to me. The baseline mindset of each child runs in a different direction. Sarah is a girl. She dresses and acts like one and lives up to the stereotype of little girls quite accurately. And Max is about as much of a boy as they can get. For a while, I used to worry about this, that somehow their mother and I were unintentionally foisting traditional gender roles upon them. I even made a point of sitting down with my daughter when she was little and watching a few Schwarzenegger films, just to see if she might get a little more aggressive.

No matter what we do, the children have decided who they are, and their genders play a part in that definition. But every now and then, the effect each has on the other comes through. My son has become quite attached to his sister's old clothes, and he has no qualms whatsoever about wearing a hand-me-down pair of pink sweatpants. On a rainy day, when the out of doors are too cold and wet to run around in, he will quite happily sit and play Barbies with his sister. He has even been known to get into his mother's mascara and lipstick.

And one day, when I walked outside, I found the two of them sitting on the porch with the box of wood scraps and the hammer and nails. Sarah was whacking away, filling an odd-looking collection of wood with a quarter of a pound of nails. I stopped her to ask what they were building. "A house for my doll," came the response, and then they went back to their work.

Call of the Wild

Okay, so I've put a great deal of effort into convincing you that I am a sensitive and caring man, a decent fellow without so much as an ounce of piggy-ness in me. I feel I should apologize here and now for lying to you about this. It is time to come clean and confess. I admit that I possess a certain amount of swinishness, a small but nevertheless measurable lump of it that nests in a corner of my brain, and every now and again, it pushes aside the cobwebs and emerges into the daylight, squealing and snorting. I want to be up front with you about that.

Now that that's taken care of, let's talk about breasts. To be more specific, let's talk about *women's* breasts. Some of you might like to talk about the sort of pseudo breasts that men have, but that's not a subject I'd care to discuss. I want to focus solely on the female kind.

Men like breasts. You female readers have probably observed this—no surprise. You men know just what I'm talking about—you, too, play host to a parasitic brain swine. I expect there are a few who do not, but as a general statement, I feel comfortable with this assertion. For many of us, the fascination with the bosom is a lifelong predilection. The male attraction to breasts begins at an early age; perhaps it is a basic instinct, or is dictated by some DNA sequence in our genetic code.

Most of us didn't recognize the attraction prior to the onslaught of puberty. But when the hormones began to tool around our systems, we noticed. We discovered that the girls no longer looked like boys, that they had these interesting bumps and rounded bits, and somewhere deep down in our tiny little animal brains the steel struck the flint and an eternal flame burst into life. The fascination drove us to great lengths, causing us to develop grand but unsuccessful schemes for peeking into the girls' locker room. The failures reduced us to unethical searches of our fathers' stuff for the latest copy of *Playboy*.

But an air-brushed, glossy photo of Miss October, no matter how scrumptious she might have looked as she watered her plants in that see-through sarong thing, was a poor substitute for the real thing. The postcard of the sunset never captures the true beauty and magic of watching the sun settle into the western sea, casting changing bands of orange and red across the clouds. We wanted the actual item, unprepared as we were for the experience. In those young and foolish times, the idea of actually seeing a real, living, breathing breast, or better still two of them, attached to a real naked lady, was enough to make most of us hyperventilate and pass out in a big hurry.

But how our views change. Now we are grown-up men, comfortable with naked ladies. Getting married or cohabiting with a woman has left most of us fairly familiar with the female breast. That is, we've probably seen a pair of them, uncovered and exposed, once or more a day. After a reasonably long marriage, we've seen a lot of that particular pair of breasts: as our beloved exits the shower, as she strips down, in preparation for donning her jammies, at the end of the day. Given that exposure, we've seen them often enough that we don't feel obliged to stare at them every single chance we get. It's not that they aren't attractive; it's just part of the process of maturing and getting more or less sensible.

The pig, though, never dies. He just nestles a little deeper into his dark corner, waiting for chances to embarrass us. Every now and then we notice the Victoria's Secret catalog, sitting out where she left it, and the pig nudges us, snorts ever so suggestively, and asks if we wouldn't perhaps like to check out all the nipples peeking through the lace in the photos. This is exactly the reason that the women's underwear section of the Sears catalog was off-limits when we were little kids.

I do not trust the pig, and I shy away from certain clothing purchases for my wife because of him. When I stroll through the ladies' section, a saleslady usually descends upon me to ask if I need help, to offer insightful suggestions. She'll often try to lead me to the racks full of articles of clothing that require me to comment on bust size. And how can I respond to this strange woman, when she shows me a beautiful blouse, a perfect color for my wife, and she asks if she is the same size as my wife? She is tempting the swine forward, asking me, nay directing me, to examine her figure, to look at her breasts.

And she is setting me up to humiliate myself and offend her. "Ma'am, you're pretty close to the same size, but my wife is bustier." Oh, that'll win some friends. I have tried, believe me, and you just cannot say things like that. Even fairly innocuous phrases like "full-figured," "chestier," and "more buxom" will get you blackballed from the department store. Although she did ask for it.

Even in life's relatively calm and mundane moments, the swine can sally forth. A woman passes by, a woman who is remarkably attractive in the chest area. Doesn't matter how she's attractive—could be she is very well-endowed, maybe not, maybe she has breasts that are a certain shape, that angle off in a particular direction. The point is, the man has found his eyes tracking from where he is supposed to be looking, say at the road, and his ears and brain disengage from all distractions, such as the conversation he has been having with his significant other, and he swivels his head violently to stare, ogle, leer, and take in this strange woman's bosom.

This is rude and occasionally dangerous. As a representative member of the male sex, let me acknowledge that our sex is aware that this is both sexist and a sign of poor upbringing. I offer my sincerest apologies to any and all women who are offended.

As men, walking around in the real world where half the people around us are women, we are confronted with a difficult choice. Avert the eyes, look at our shoes, walk into doors and walls. Or listen to the pig in our heads screaming "Check out the hooters on her!" and let him loose to cop the occasional side-long glance. Take your choice. Unless we can train ourselves to safely ignore or be neutral toward the breasts around us, we'll either end up looking like klutzes or being insensitive morons. It is a thickly sown minefield we males tread, and all too often we are in the brown stuff up to our ankles—head first.

But I can tell you right now, it isn't going to stop any time soon. Even as I recognize the callous, piggy side of my sex, I am still firm in my opinion that breasts are wonderful. The shape and form of the breast is really quite nice. This construction of tissue has a graceful aspect, an attractive demeanor, and can serve a useful function, as in feeding a baby. Truly, breasts are marvelous things. It is rare for something to be both beautiful and functional, and have such potential to get me in such hot water with my spouse.

The only solution is compromise. I try not to stare at other women when my wife is around. And she has the decency to avoid long, lingering looks at men with really good butts.

My One True Love

I saw a Toyota zip past me on the freeway the other day, with a license plate that read TRU LUV. A nice thought that, unless it refers to the driver's affection for the car, which would be more indicative of a misplaced sense of values. I'd like to believe that it means that the driver has a husband or boyfriend or significant other who really feels that way about her, and that the license or the car was a token of affection.

It's a pleasant idea that somewhere out there, among the other five-plus billion human beings, there is your one true love. A perfect soul, matched to yours, ready for a lifelong state of bliss. All you have to do is find him or her.

Good luck. It probably isn't going to happen.

Let's talk in real world terms. Even if you could somehow magically identify that special person, you can't choose from all five billion. They just aren't within arm's reach, never mind small issues like language and cultural barriers. So you just can't assume that you can select from the entire population of the world. Let's cut that pool down to a group that you may have a lot in common with, say the residents of these United States of America. That means only 260,000,000 souls, give or take a few. Again, this is too large an area to work from. So let's say that you limit yourself to your immediate environment, which I will assume to be a relatively good-sized metropolitan area, with a population of 5,000,000. But you won't be selecting from this entire population. It is safe to assume that your interest is in only one of the sexes. Whether you are straight or gay, then, there are only 2,500,000 people to choose from.

Next you had better reduce that to some range of age that is reasonable, as well as legal. For sake of argument, assume only 30 percent are in a range acceptable to you, which then lowers the available number to 750,000. And, some of those 750,000 folk are going to be married, attached, disinterested, or otherwise unavailable, so let's cut out another 500,000.

Now your love pool is a mere 250,000. You are hoping that somewhere in that one quarter of one million people is one person who is absolutely and utterly perfect for you. Likes to sit on the sofa and drink beer and watch football, or go to the opera and cry through the diva's finest performance, or whatever else you'd like Mister or Miz Right to be into.

If you figure that you have to check out each one of them personally, and you can work out a way to date all of them to see for yourself, then you're talking about a date every night of the week, including holidays, for 684.931 years. Which is, of course, impractical. Even if you got really lucky and only had to try 10 percent of them before you found the right mate, you're still faced with over sixty-five years worth of dating, and if you paid for dinner, a tab of around a million bucks, not including tax and tip. And then you'd have to wonder if any of the remaining 90 percent might be an even better fit.

When you glance over at your significant other, sitting propped up in bed reading a Jackie Collins novel, are you now wondering if you may have made a horrible mistake? Is there someone out there suffering to the very depth of heart and soul because you happen to be married to someone else? Considering the numbers and facts I've just presented you with, you now realize that short of an act of God, you'll probably never find that person. Considering all the variations and vagaries of human beings, it is actually nothing short of a miracle that the two right people ever get together at all.

But somehow a huge number of us do marry or commit to long term relationships. We find love and happiness in a person who may not have the *Playboy* or *Playgirl* body, who lacks the sophistication of *GQ*'s cover guy, who does not make a hundred jillion dollars a year. We settle for someone who we may sometimes disagree with, fight with, or just flat out get really ticked off at from time to time. Considering the odds against it, it seems pretty amazing that so many of us find love, settle down, have kids, get married, or make long-term commitments. But it's a good thing that we do—if we all held out for the ultimate match, the human species would have died out in one or two generations.

The underlying message must be a tribute to the flexibility and adaptability of the human animal. The fact that there are so many happily joined couples out there says something about the nature of love, that it is not an absolute requiring a certain set of criteria to be met, but that love and a good relationship are based on patience and compromise, an agreement to work together even when you'd like to flush the toilet while your wife is in the shower.

I was looking for true love. In the five or six years I dated before I got married, I may have gone out with all of thirty or forty different women. Most of those were one date only, as it was immediately obvious that we weren't meant for each other. In terms of longer spans, say ten or more dates, maybe five or six of them would count. Of all of the women I dated, I thought I was in love with two, and knew that I was in love with one, who fortunately turned out to my wife. As luck would have it, she was also in love with me, so getting married seemed like a reasonable idea.

Was it true love then? Is it true love now? Is my marriage that one-in-a-horribly-large-number that really is the blessed state, conferred upon mortals by the powers that be? Are we the perfect match?

No. If there is a couple out there enraptured in true love of mythical proportions, we aren't it. The powers that be did not point down from the heavens and tap us as the shining example of what love is meant to be. We have fights, rare but very real, and while I love being with Marie, there are moments when I am quite content to hang out by myself. It is a love that is real-world and practical even while it is romantic. True love strikes me as blind to the realities of the world, like paying bills and taking the trash out, and must be a lot like smoking laughing tobacco.

I still like the *idea* of a perfect love. My children believe in it, courtesy of all the fairy tales they've heard. I confess that I also get a little choked up when I read to them about the pure and absolute love at first sight between the long-suffering princess and the handsome prince. But if you want to know what I really think, I'd hazard a guess that Prince Charming probably slept on the royal couch more than once.

The Old Ball
and Chain

A book with stories like these wouldn't be complete if it didn't have at least one about falling in love and getting married. How could I tell you about being a kid and having kids if I don't tell you about the intermediate stage, the thing that came in between?

Well, it started this way: There was this knockout redhead that worked for the same company I did. Her tresses were not deep red or the auburn red, but that color that is sort of a glorious wash of red and blond. I've been a sucker for red hair ever since I was a kid and saw "I Love Lucy" in color for the first time.

But I've always been a little shy with women, so I tried to contrive some reason or "chance meeting" to talk to her, rather than just introducing myself outright. After a week of trying, I finally managed to put myself in front of her at the copy machine. My mind is a sieve when it comes to remembering names, and I forgot hers about two minutes after she told me what it was. It was a bit odd to think about her as often as I did, without a name—just as the "redhead." But I was too embarrassed to tell her that I had forgotten, and instead I asked someone else. I repeated it to myself over and over again in a singsong way—Marie, Marie, Marie, Marie, Marie—until it was as firmly locked into my brain as a mantra.

I kept thinking about her, and about asking her out. One evening at quitting time, I was walking out the back door to go home, and I passed her coming the other way. I said hello and started to walked on past. But the smarter half of my brain told the shy half to sit down and shut up and let it do the talking. I stopped and turned around, and called after her.

"Would you be offended if I asked you out Friday night?" My smooth, ultra-cool pick-up line showed a level of humility and a complete lack of self-confidence that women just love.

"I can't Friday," was her reply, and I immediately assumed that here I was barking up the wrong tree again. I imagined that she had a boyfriend named Steve, and that he was built like a tank, and she'd say how flattered she was that I'd asked, but Steve wouldn't like it if she went out with me, even for a "friendly" date. Steve would probably feel it necessary to kill me, or break my legs at least. But then she said, "How about next Friday instead? You see, I'm moving this weekend, so I'm kind of busy."

And that sealed the date. The appointed evening, April first, I got duded up in my best suit and set off for her house, getting lost twice and pulled over once (for a busted tail light). We went out for Japanese food, and ate sukiyaki and drank sake, and I had a perfect time. I didn't try to kiss her. Just the handshake at her front door, a comment on what a nice time I'd had, and a quiet but thoughtful drive home.

On our second date, I was invited in for coffee. We sat in her living room and talked. She told me about her parents, and growing up in Redding and Southern California, and how she happened to come to Seattle. And I told her about my family and traveling in Africa, and I taught her a word or two of Swahili. The coffee that she offered never materialized. She left it sitting on the counter until it was stone cold. But I didn't mind. I finally saddled up and headed for home about one o'clock in the morning, feeling good about the date, and planning to ask her out again.

Almost every weekend thereafter we went out. We seemed to click. She laughed at my jokes and foolish behavior, and I loved everything about her—her brains, her beauty, the sound of her voice when she sang, and her ability to see a solution when everything was collapsing in a heap of confusion. Slowly it dawned on me that I was in trouble, because every time I asked her for a date, she said yes. And finally, one evening, she said that I wasn't leaving until I kissed her good night. I began to understand that something had changed in my life. I was in love, really and truly, and I told her so. I meant it, understood what it meant, and more than anything else in the world, I wanted her to feel the same way and say the same words to me.

At one point or another in growing up, most everyone thinks they are in love at least once. As a teenager, I thought I was a couple of times. I wasn't. True, the feelings I felt were pretty strong, and when a girl broke up with me, I thought I was going to keel over and die. But there was no past experience that carried anything like the intensity of falling in love with Marie. Her existence affected my life.

I met Marie's parents and friends, and I decided that I liked her family a lot. A couple of weeks later, it occurred to me that I really wanted this relationship to go on for a long time—that I would like to marry her. I asked her what she might think if I were to propose to her. I didn't want to just out and out ask; I wanted to get her opinion first. And in the fashion that I have since come to know is her way, she told me that if I wanted to know what she thought, I would have to ask her and find out.

I decided that further study was needed. Two weeks later, I proposed to her on the steps of Terry Hall at the University of Washington, with a box of leftover pizza from our dinner under my arm. And miraculously, she said yes.

At this point, all of the wedding stuff kicked into gear. Telling parents and gauging their reactions, some good, some not, picking dresses and bride's maids and groom's guys, cakes and all that. Even though we were engaged for almost a year, the feeling of anticipation and romance was intoxicating.

I could tell you in great detail the highlights of the wedding—the music and vows and the reception, and all the other stuff that goes with it. The fact that we paid off the minister with a twelve-year-old bottle of Scotch. That we exited to the *1812 Overture,* complete with a cannon fired in the parking lot. That for our honeymoon, we stayed in a posh hotel in Seattle, and had dinner at a fine restaurant, where a strolling guitarist serenaded us with a flamenco version of "Tie Me Kangaroo Down." And how we drove to Canada and ate river trout and red cabbage and spätzle at a German hofbrau owned by a Vietnamese family.

It was a fine and interesting experience. I had a good time. But the micro details of any wedding are only really important to the participants. Suffice to say that it was fun, and it was one of the two or three weddings that I have attended that I actually was sorry to see end.

The wedding was over a decade ago now. Sometimes I pause and think about what has happened in that span of time, where we have been and what we have done. That we have two children, a mortgage on a house that needs a paint job in the worst sort of way, pets and joint checking accounts. In the intervening years, we have found more common ground than differences, we have learned new things together (although I never thought she'd want to learn to scuba dive). As we have grown and matured together, I find that there is more about her to love—I find I love her more now than in the beginning. And she still laughs at my jokes, and I still love to hear her sing. I would rather spend time with her than anyone else. My idea of heaven is an evening out with her, just the two of us.

I like to remind her of that every so often. I like to send her flowers on the occasions that I am not supposed to, like our 10.3 anniversary, or Saint Wiggen's Day. The important thing is to send the message that I love her all the time, that I tell her all the time, not just on the required days like Valentine's. And besides, it's cheaper to send flowers during non-events—they raise the price of flowers for Valentine's.

I wear one piece of jewelry, my wedding ring. Over a decade ago, it was a perfectly round band, with a brushed finish that was subtle, understated. A small inscription circles the inside with my wife's message of love for me. Now the matte finish has been polished away to a scratched, shiny surface; the ring is no longer round but slightly ovoid from the years of banging and abuse. And the finger upon which it lives has a trench at the base where the finger meets my palm. The ring, like me, is a little beat up, showing its age and all the miles that have been passed.

But the inscription is still there, and every so often I take the ring off, to rediscover the message. Simply: "H. I love you. M."—written in Swahili.

Terrorists and Other Small Children

I'd like to introduce you to my son, Hayden Maxwell Fulghum, the international terrorist in training. His agent is already discussing terms of his future employment with the PLO, the IRA, and several other groups and cells bent on world destruction, release of political prisoners, nuclear explosions in Washington, DC, and other such questionable activities. There's no doubt in my mind that he'll be a first-round choice: "The Brigada Rosa takes as its first pick in the 2010 terrorist draft . . . Max Fulghum, a nuclear bomb specialist from Terror University."

His paternal grandfather says that Max is sweet revenge upon me for all the trouble I caused, just as I was my grandfather's revenge upon my father. My nickname at church for many years was the Holy Terror, a title I lived up to with great relish. I suspect a genetic link that must go back many generations, and considering family history, may have been to blame for the Civil War. Of course, I cannot prove this, but I suspect it very strongly.

Having a son can be so completely different from having a daughter. Yes, I admit that it sounds sexist, but the male child is quite frankly much more aggressive. Our family doctor says that it is testosterone poisoning, and that it cannot be cured, only controlled. Max makes guns, wants to drive bomber airplanes, and likes toy soldiers. He and his two best buddies at school have decided that when they grow up, they will get a super-fast fighter airplane, so that they can drive it over to the bad guys' houses and drop bombs on them, which will 'splode and make the bad guys go away. Or at very least make them feel bad about being bad guys and say that they are sorry and will become good guys.

Everything in my boy's life can be reduced to good guys doing right, and bad guys doing wrong. Sounds a lot like the foreign policy of the Reagan administration if you ask me. Naive, but easy to understand.

Now, being modern parents, my wife and I are very much of the opinion that toy guns and other toys of aggression are *bad*. We lecture the children, saying no pows, booms, or kerwhooshes. It isn't nice to shoot at people, even if it's play. Guns are *bad* things. And I try to explain to Max that driving a plane over to a bad guy's house to drop bombs on it isn't a very friendly thing to do. There is no need to explain this to Sarah; she instinctively knows this to be true.

There is some relief when Max assures me patiently and quite earnestly that this is all pretend, a harmless fantasy, and that the bad guys see the light and become much nicer. No damage or death occurs. Too bad the real world doesn't work that way.

I got to thinking about this issue the other day. I have heard from a number of sources that toy guns and that ilk of plaything are not healthy. They encourage violence and a gamelike attitude toward death and murder. You've probably been part of the debate. The average child watches so many murders and killings in an average day that their average little brains are unable to distinguish between the reality of death and the imaginary type presented on TV. And what about all these horribly violent video games, with guts and limbs and viscera flying? What are *those* teaching our children? The conventional wisdom is that all this exposure to violence is a really bad thing, and I'd better watch out or my child will do horrible things when he grows up.

Really?

I think back to my parents and my own upbringing. At first, my parents forbade any sort of war toy or gun in the house. Not that it did any good—my brother and I didn't need weapons to fight and tussle. This led to obvious confusion for the adults. If we were raised in a household without war toys, why were we so aggressive? The family doctor made the observation that some of our behavior was normal, that withholding toys wasn't really a solution, and that a child need only point a finger and say "bang" to have a toy gun. And my parents caved in at that.

At which point, my childhood became more or less normal for the time. We played Batman and Gunsmoke and had pop guns, Daisy BB guns and cap guns and toy army suits, and a heap of GI Joes, and a Bangsite cannon. The gang that I ran around with after school—David, Timothy and Christopher—

spent our afternoons in the woods, building tiger traps and blowing up Japanese and German soldiers, those Dirty "Japs" and Dirty "Krauts"—at least that's what the Duke called 'em. Our favorite part, pretending to die after being mowed down by a sneaky enemy in a hidden machine gun nest, involved rolling down the slope above the backyard, throwing pine-cone grenades at our killers, and fighting for America to the end. Patton would have been proud. We had all manner of toy guns, both store-bought and homemade; we were armed to the teeth. And did we ever get into trouble. Like the time I tossed a brick through the front window of the vacant house next door. All the neighborhood kids were trying to figure out how to get in and play, and we couldn't. So I busted the largest and most expensive window in the house.

The experts these days would expect me to have grown up to be a real psycho, with an AK-47 in the trunk of my car and a "My Wife, Yes, My Dog, Maybe, My Gun, Never" bumper sticker on the pickup. But that didn't happen. And none of the other demons from the seventh level of hell that I played with wound up in jail or on the wrong end of a pistol. As far as I know, none of them beat their spouses or children, and all seem to be reasonably nice guys.

So maybe my terror-child Max isn't apt to end up in real trouble, either. In truth, he is a fine kid, my good buddy and best friend, capable of moments of gentleness that are truly wonderful to behold.

But just the other day, he asked me a rather complicated question about nuclear fusion, and after I had explained, I asked why he wanted to know. And he wouldn't tell me. He just smiled.

Christmas

I am reminded from time to time of the Christmas I spent manning the Salvation Army kettle at a Lynnwood department store many years ago. The adults rang the bell. My job, as the four-year-old waif in Osh Kosh overalls, was to plaintively ask the shoppers rushing in and out to ". . . please help the *poor* people!" We always did well.

This charitable excursion, and others like it, became a part of my family's Christmas tradition. My years with the Salvation Army provided childhood memories that I cherish.

Now that I have grown up, my wife has taken over as charity point person in the household. One of the annual holiday events around our house is making a Christmas basket for a needy family. Marie gathers all the particulars about the family (clothing sizes and "wish lists" are provided by the sponsors) and then she goes shopping. She returns from these trips with the backseat of her car laden with booty, and an ever so subtle glint in her eye.

As the stash gets assembled in the dining room, the house takes on an added sense of Christmas. I've always found Christmas wrapping to be a bother, but as Marie wraps the gifts and adds bows and ribbons, I enjoy seeing the parcels begin to collect.

Last year, Marie ended up with three boxes (and I mean *big* boxes—two feet on a side) filled with food and two bags filled with gifts, wrapped and tagged: "To so and so, from Santa." I wasn't much help. It had been another busy season at the office, and the holidays moved up on me much too quickly for my own comfort. For the most part, my involvement was to stay out of the way. By the time I even thought to offer to help, everything was ready to go. There was one thing I could do, though. I could deliver the boxes and bags to the distribution center, Thursday morning, before ten. No problem.

I loaded the three fifty-pound boxes and two bags of presents into the back of my car. And I drove to Bothell, sure I'd be there before the families arrived. I'd simply drop off the donation, get a receipt, and be on my way assured that we had done a nice thing. I sang "Away in a Manger" and "Deck the Hall" all the way there.

Everything was going to be wonderful. Except that, in fact, people had been lined up at the center for at least an hour before I arrived. There were more than a hundred of them, standing in the parking lot in an awful, drizzly rain, waiting for a little Christmas cheer. Sad-looking people. Lots of mothers with small, wet children, elderly folk, and more than a few who looked like they hadn't seen too many regular meals of late.

And I show up to deliver the last donation. No one else was coming after me. Even worse, I have to park in front of all these people to unload my car. My new car. Wearing my hundred-dollar loafers, pressed slacks, dress shirt, coat, and tie. I was probably wearing clothes worth twice the cost of the donation.

The last thing I wanted to do was to make these people feel bad. I sure didn't want them to think I had come to see them, to gloat, to be better than they were. But I had to deliver the donation. A man helping with the unloading and dispersal grabbed a hand cart and told me that we needed to be as fast as we could. He didn't want me to make them feel bad, either.

The whole situation made me feel rotten. Rotten about Christmas, myself, charity, the whole ball of wax. Here I am, delivering a gift that is supposed to make someone's Christmas a little better, and I end up feeling like a complete jerk. Wonderful. Merry Stinking Christmas, ho-ho-ho.

Let me ask you this. Faced with this situation, what would you have done? This classifies as one of those nightmares about being naked at school. There is no easy way out. Would you have apologized to everyone, or averted your eyes, or pretended that you weren't really there?

I'll tell you what I did. I bent over and picked up a box. In my loafers, pressed slacks, dress shirt, coat, and tie. In my slacks that are a little too tight across the backside. Yup, I bent over and ripped the seat out of my pants. And not a little rip. No way. I gutted those pants. Tore them from crotch to belt line, with an audible *rrrrriiiiippp*. In front of all those people.

I cringed for a moment. Then I picked up that box, and I marched inside and delivered it with my boxers hanging out. But as I went inside, you know what I heard? Laughter. Those people were laughing. And in spite of my embarrassment, I laughed, too. All the way into the center, all the way out, and all the way home to change my pants.

I guess I gave those people an extra present that wasn't on the list or in the boxes or bags. A little laughter for Christmas, at the right time, to take the edge off the indignity, to make the day a little lighter, to stop the sadness for a minute or two.

Marie has mended the pants for me. As she was sewing them up, she asked if maybe she hadn't ought to let them out a little. Not a chance. When I deliver next year's donation, I'll wear them again.

F.A.O.
Schwarzenegger

It was that time again. The holiday season, which these days starts around Halloween, had brought festive displays of fake snow and cheery Saint Nicks winking from the store windows. My duty as Santa Dad required that I participate in the celebration of the birth of the Christ Child through the purchasing of consumer goods.

I was walking through F.A.O. Schwarz right before closing time. I stopped to buy a Power Ranger action figure for child number two and a Barbie dress for child number one. The clerk was red-eyed, cheeks a bit hollow, with the hint of stubble. He looked worn through.

"Tough day?" I asked.

"Terrible," he said. "I am sick of it."

"Sick of what?"

"That damn song. Every kid who has walked though the

doors in the last eight hours has insisted on pressing the button, and that damn song plays and plays and plays. I hate Christmas. All these kids come in and play that damn song."

In the front entrance of the store sat a large, happy-looking tree, smiling a broad, toothy grin. Two big red buttons on its side beckoned, and if you pressed the first one, the tree told you in a warm and friendly voice just how happy it was to see you, oh joy-joy-joy! Nearby, the irresistible candy-colored button number two waited, ready to start the dreaded song: "Welcome to our world, welcome to our world, welcome to our world of toys. Welcome to our world, welcome to our world" and so on, over and over.

The clerk was fingering a sharpened #2 pencil and watching a small cherub dressed in Osh Kosh overalls and Mickey Mouse shoes, socks, and shirt, toddling towards the button, a bit of spittle beginning to stretch from the lower lip into a long strand of gooh. The clerk watched with the anticipation of those damned to small tortures and, as the button was pressed by small, sticky fingers, the clerk winced audibly, the bones in his neck crackling out a percussive start to "Welcome to our world, welcome to our world."

I left the store in a hurry, fleeing the spreading stain of Christmas cynicism. I understand the clerk's burden. I have found that much as I love the fluff and ribbons and holiday spirit, the lights and music and the general sense of goodwill, the *amount* of Christmas that I am force-fed by the world at large is just too much. Retailers deck their stores out as winter scenes—complete with home stereo equipment for that special someone. Gnomes sing fa-la-la-la-la, smiling gaily, and wondering if I wouldn't like to buy a quart of anti-freeze for my beloved.

Christmas cards arrive from friends, relatives, insurance sales-man, the chiropractor, the auto service center, the magazines I got subscriptions to last Christmas (all reminding me that I need to renew), and Heaven knows who else.

The whole thing is an assault on my senses by the Santa Shock troops, wishing me, nay, *telling* me, to have a merry ho-ho. By December 26, I will be profoundly grateful that we have a modest breather before Easter.

If it is hard for me, I can only imagine the way the clerks must feel. I am exposed to the mall at my convenience, and cer-tainly not for more than eight or ten hours in a Christmas sea-son. I can go home, lock my door, turn on a CD of Don Ho, and escape from the aspartame sweetness of the most commercial time of the year. I have a choice to participate to whatever de-gree I choose. But imagine a forty-hour work week, eight hours a day, from Halloween 'til late December, listening to "Deck the Hall" and "Away in a Manger," forced not only to be nice to the customers but also to maintain a cheery disposition while a line twenty-five deep forms at your till. Imagine having to deal with tired, angry, strung-out shoppers, all driving full bore to D day, the 25th of December.

The clerk at F.A.O. Schwarz had obviously reached the end of his particular rope. I could picture him coming in to start his shift decked out in surplus fatigues, a Vulcan 30-millimeter mini-cannon, loaded for small children and parental escort slung over his weary shoulder: "Tragedy at the mall today. Fif-teen dead, film at eleven."

Since the holidays are about love and kindness and warmth and family, I think we should all back off a couple of notches, cut down on the gifts a bit, mellow out, and savor the moments.

Take ten deep breaths next time you rush through the mall, enjoy the carols, drop five bucks in the kettle. Smile and wish strangers a Happy Holiday.

And if fate or your shopping list should cause you to arrive at F.A.O. Schwarz during the Christmas season, no matter what else you do, don't press the buttons.

January

January is here, and I have begun the process of dismembering Christmas.

A stack of flattened boxes to be recycled sits neatly by the door, the ornaments are nestled in leftover red and green tissue, packed and ready to be stored in the back of the closet until next year. A fire kindled with wrapping paper and fueled with Christmas tree logs burns in the hearth, the colored paper flaring briefly in jets of blue and red.

The long, remorseless descent through autumn into winter is complete, and while the days begin to get longer in ever-so-small slices, the anticipation of Christmas and the New Year are no longer there to distract me from the cold and the deep, wet darkness outside the living room window. I stand watching the rain and the gray and the unraked leaves, and I feel the weight of winter. Even fireside, I feel the chill to my soul.

This is January, when winter truly sets in on my mind. The time of waiting for any sign of green, the first crocus, or a hint of the sun to warm the air just enough to remind me of spring. On cold, crisp, sunny days, I pause and hold my cheek to the sun, eyes closed, remembering summer, as I feel that slight bit of warmth. My wife occasionally catches me doing this, and I tell her that I am photosynthesizing. This is a time to make resolutions about the future, to catch one's breath after the brouhaha of the holiday has receded, and before the horror of the VISA bill hits. January brings on a siege mentality, bundled as I am into the house, in the midst of leftover Christmas cards and Super Bowl hype.

January has always left me with a sense of emptiness, of gloom. Post-Christmas depression, the let down from the bull rush to the holiday, winter fatigue, just plain cold and dark—whatever the cause, I look forward to its end. I savor the lead-in to Christmas, and I dread the aftermath.

This year, the time before Christmas was spent with Jewish friends, cutting a tree from a mucky field, riding on a tractor back to the truck, on a rainbow road made from thousands of pounds of broken and polished colored glass, snacking on cider and cookies—Norman Rockwell couldn't have painted it better. The next day, we gathered to hang lights and ornaments and tinsel. We traded jokes about heathen holiday practices, and the risk of having non-believers in the house, but deep down, these friends were a special part of our Christmas. We pulled out all of the boxes of decorations and spread them from one end of the house to the other, hanging wreathes and garlands, and covering the mantle with fresh boughs. The house was filled with a scent of Scotch pine and Doug fir that no air freshener can match. One of our friends' children, now four, had never decorated a tree before, and the wonder and confusion of beautiful wood and glass ornaments put her in rapture. Time and time again, she told me in her small lisping voice that there was a *tree! In my house!*

The child's father and I tried to explain the differences between Christmas and Chanukah to all of the children, when it suddenly occurred to me that I had no idea why I celebrate Christmas. I am somewhere between Atheist and Agnostic, and I have always held doubts about the person Jesus Christ. I found myself wondering what was I doing, celebrating the birth of someone I don't believe in.

Christmas is a lot of things to a lot of people. At its most fundamental, Christmas is the celebration of the birth of Jesus Christ, timed closely to the beginning of winter—as though the deliverance of God's only son unto Mankind was granted at the time of greatest darkness and deepest fear. The sun and warmth and life are furthest from us, and a child of God arrives, with the promise that life will return.

Someone once told me that they had heard that Jesus was born in October, which might make him a libra. The idea that the Son of God would be born under the astrological sign of balance pleases me. It seems fitting. It's been said that we celebrate in December to obscure older pagan rituals tied to the winter solstice and replace them with the Christian ones, much as the tradition of a Christmas tree—the evergreen representing eternal life and the promise of spring.

This Christmas, my children turned a corner in their celebration of the holiday. They were caught up in a whirlwind of joy, and they decided to leave gifts for Santa Claus. Precious personal belongings—a sparkly pencil, a pair of Mickey Mouse sunglasses, a favorite wooden truck—were wrapped in far too much paper and sealed with far too much tape. We cut out snowflakes and lots of Christmas dinosaurs, and the children carefully set everything before the altar of Santa, the fireplace. A plate of homemade Christmas cookies and a glass of eggnog were added to round out the gift, along with a bunch of nine carrots, peeled by the children, for the reindeer (one for each, including Rudolf).

The remarkable thing about this orgy of selflessness was that it was entirely spontaneous. We had not prompted the children at all. They just did it. They had discovered the joy of giving, as simple and sappy as that may seem. It is a fundamental idea that is difficult, even as an adult, to understand.

So what does Christmas mean to me?

It is not religion. Jesus may have been born, possibly in October, for the salvation of Man, but not for me. And not Santa. Santa may exist for some, but I know better. We may celebrate to mark the beginning of the end of winter, but I do not need to hang tinsel and colored lights to make the sun come back.

Christmas is about all of these things and none of them. For me, it is being close with family and friends, it's taking care to express the love and affection I feel, that perhaps I forget to share during the year. It is being with my Jewish friends for an evening of warmth. It is watching my children learn the joy of giving. If I celebrate Christmas for no other reason, let it be the moment to wish to each other Happiness and Joy and Health. Let it stand as a moment of love, at the end of the darkness, at the end of the year, in preparation for spring and what lies beyond.

In the depth of the winter, I feel a slight spark of comfort and light, a small ember still burning from Christmas. I shelter it from the cold wind of winter, and feed it bits of tinder and wood, knowing that it will keep me warm just as I care for it.

Merry January.

A Whack to
the Head

I was having lunch with Elizabeth, when she turned the subject to children. A rookie wife with only a year or so of wedded bliss under her belt, she lacks the wisdom that comes with the ten-plus years of matrimony that I can lay claim to. Poor confused thing. Elizabeth is pondering the life choices related to children, and with little experience to go on, she's making decisions in a vacuum. Always glad to offer advice when none is asked for, I enumerated the three rules about children that I have found to be true.

Rule number one is the "Law of Time." Simply stated, after the first child, the amount of time you must devote to your children never changes, no matter how many you may have. Impossible, you say. Ah, well, you see, one child takes all of your time. Two children also take all of your time. As do three, and four, and so on. You see my point. More children means more laundry and more diapers and more midnight feedings, but it doesn't necessarily mean more time. You have no more to give.

The second is the "Rule of Infinites." To be an effective parent, you must have infinite patience and infinite interest. Since this is theoretically impossible, you must strive to come as close as possible and, realizing that you will fail, accept the consequences as entirely your fault.

The third and final rule of children is very simple, and absolutely as unhelpful as it can possibly be. In a nutshell, parenting is one of those "sign-here-don't-read-the-fine-print" deals. It requires a leap of faith, because there is no way of knowing what you are getting into. Even being a parent doesn't prepare you for being a parent. One child can be as different from another as day is from night—and usually is. The rule is: Expect anything.

Truly, the biggest challenge upon becoming a parent stems from the lack of understanding and information. None of your previous life experience will have prepared you to any real degree. You may have taken classes, read books, attended lectures, even been present for the birth of a child, yours or anybody else's. But everything up until the baby emerges from the birth canal is pure theory. The aftermath, in the form of a child, is a mysterious bundle of potential whose circuits are wired up in whatever fashion they happen to be. It is a bit like skydiving. All the practice in the world won't prepare you for the moment when you first stand in the door of the airplane, five thousand feet above the earth. The only difference is when you're skydiving, you don't have to jump if you don't want to.

As a first-time parent, I discovered that my level of ignorance about babies and their needs was rather embarrassing. I have never quite figured out how a person of moderate intelligence could grow up and learn about sex without learning about the consequences of it, intended or not. Upon the arrival of our first child, we were so overwhelmed by the wonderful new addition to our family, a beautiful little girl, that we had little sense of the bomb that was about to detonate in our household. This feeling was soon replaced by a stunned sense of utter confusion, not unlike discovering that all the instructions for one's new stereo system are written in fourteenth-century Mandarin Chinese.

Being a starter parent introduced me to all levels of ignorance. Babies are inherently designed to make one feel inadequate and foolish. I discovered that I hadn't a clue about diapers, bottles, or those midnight strolls down the hall with a crying child.

The day Sarah came home from the hospital, we assumed (there's that word) that she'd do fine on breast milk, and therefore that we had all the equipment we needed—two breasts, both busily lactating away. That turned out to be a rather dumb assumption to make, and was compounded by having no baby formula, and a grand total of one—count 'em—bottle and rubber nipple in the whole house.

Sarah was what the nurse at the hospital called a "bad latcher" and a "lazy nurser." She had a rough time getting a good hold on a nipple. And if she actually did latch on, the wonderful calming effect of warm milk in her tummy made her so wonderfully content, she'd fall asleep almost immediately. The nurse who coached us before we left the hospital said to tickle Sarah to keep her awake, lift her arms up over her head, and be very, very patient. Nursing could prove to be an arduous task, a two-person job—Marie to handle logistics, me to harass Sarah and keep her awake.

That first day passed uneventfully, and the three of us retired for the evening, still in the glow of it all. Sarah nestled in her crib, Marie and I cozied up together in our bed. Everything was calm and quiet.

And then the bomb hit. Two A.M., general quarters alarm—baby in need of breast feeding—all hands on deck, man your battle stations! I staggered down the hall, retrieved Sarah, and propped her up with my wife to eat. But it just didn't work. Marie's breasts were so swollen with milk that Sarah couldn't get a good hold of either nipple. No matter how hard we tried, the child couldn't or wouldn't latch on. And the harder we tried, the more Sarah wailed. We finally gave up on the idea, and I loaded up a bottle with cow's milk and microwaved it. A little too long, as it turns out. I set the nipple on fire. It smoked and smoldered, leaving a pool of oozing latex in the center of the microwave. So Sarah got louder and hungrier. We tried pacifiers and a lot of walking, until she finally cried herself to sleep.

At 7:58 A.M. the following morning, I was on the front steps of the pharmacy, rattling the door at the people within and pointing at my watch. I must have looked a sight, as I had no sleep, no shower, and no shave. I picked up more bottles and lots more nipples, and a breast pump, and whisked them home as fast as I could. I still don't know why I didn't buy some formula. Sleep deprivation? Maybe just out and out stupidity.

The first order of business was to pump off a little milk, to relieve the pressure that Marie was feeling, and to get the milk into Sarah as fast as possible. With a little fumbling, we got the pump to work, and Sarah got some food in her tummy. All was well with the world, and I went off to work for a couple of hours, knowing that my wife and child were now fine. Or so I thought, foolish soul that I am.

I got home a little after lunch, to find Sarah lying on our bed, howling, and my wife swearing like a teamster in between sobs and sniffs. The pump wasn't working, and both of them had reached the end of their rope. As it turned out, there was a small rubber O-ring in the pump that needed to be wet in order to get a good seal, and thereby create some suction. After we figured that out, all really was well with the world.

Parenting is unpredictable, and far from easy, but it can be a joyful learning experience. Most of the things that you need to know may be hinted at by those more experienced in the art of mommy- and daddyhood, or suggested by those handbooks that they give you before you leave the hospital. But in truth, you need to live it to learn to be a good parent. Even if that means doing a few stupid things like setting Playtex nipples on fire.

The experience, setting the nipple on fire and all, taught me a good lesson. It made me realize that I was pretty much an ignoramus when it came to children, and that I should proceed with caution. My second child, Max, only reinforced the feeling that each child was a new challenge. Sure, I know how to hold a baby, how to bathe a child. But that ability doesn't mean I know how to hold or bathe *this* baby.

Recently my elder brother, Christian, called to tell me I was going to be an uncle. The fact that he has a stepdaughter makes him think that he knows something about children. I will be glad to impart as much of my experience as I can to my brother, but I know that I can't simply pass along everything that I know about children. You can't do a brain dump; it just doesn't work that way. But there is one small thing I can do for him that may save him a bit of unhappiness. My baby shower present to him and his wife will be a simple one. One can of formula, one bottle, and two nipples.

I Have Seen the Enemy and He Is Me

1977. Her Parents' House

I had scrubbed up and put on my cleanest and nicest clothes, for this all-important meeting. After dating her for four weeks, her father has requested that I stop by a little early, before our date, so he can get to know me. I've got my company manners ready, and I even took my earring out.

Her mother greets me at the door, explaining that her daughter will be ready in a moment. In the meantime, I can wait in the den. She shows me the way, and then excuses herself.

I have the place to myself for a few moments, so I examine the room. Her dad is ex-navy, a retired commander or captain, I think. Even if I hadn't known that, the den would have given me a clue. There is a photograph of a younger man—her father—in full dress with a pretty healthy collec-

tion of medals and ribbons on his chest. The walls have several photographs of a destroyer, and in a display case behind the desk is a beautiful model of the same ship. Just as I am examining it, he walks in.

A perfect opening. I love models and ships, and I immediately begin asking him about the ship and his experience. He is stand-offish, and answers a few questions before he begins to interrogate me. Where are we going, how are we getting there, is it a party and will there be alcohol? I give him all the answers I can, and where he covers dangerous areas, like the bit about alcohol, I lie my ass off. "No sir, none of that." After a while, he just looks into my eyes. I feel really nervous, and I can tell he is trying to get some sense of me, to decide to trust me with his daughter or not.

In the end, he lets us go, with an admonishment about being home in decent season. And being careful. He isn't talking about my driving, either.

2001. My Den

I have been here before. Many years ago, I stood in a den like this, waiting for her father. Now, I am the father, and I can hear the boy approaching.

He enters the room, his eyes looking around, taking in the dark-wood paneling, dark wing-back chairs, a fire crackling in the hearth, and the many, many guns in the glass-fronted cabinet behind my desk. I seat the young man in a low, uncomfortable chair, and lean back in my own.

"Son," I say, holding up a pistol, "this is a 9-millimeter Walther PPK. Beautiful, isn't it?" He does not respond, not knowing where the conversation is leading. "It has a short

range but impressive stopping power. One or two hits in the torso, and it's all over.

"This," I add, holding up a larger weapon, "is a .44 Magnum. Reasonably accurate, when loaded with Black Talon bullets, these bad boys will shred your innards just like that." Snapping my fingers for emphasis, I see that I have his attention.

I continue. "I want to be straight with you. You seem like a nice young fellow, and my little girl likes you well enough. But I am not so far away from thirteen that I do not understand your interest in my daughter. So let me be frank. If you lay a finger on her, I'll kill you. If you hurt her, I'll kill you. If anything bad happens to her while she's with you, I'll kill you. Now," I say, smiling as I usher him to the door, "the two of you go out and have a nice time."

1995. Here and Now

Every so often, I recall the first scene. And more frequently, I imagine the second. Some day, I will be that father, meeting my daughter's dates. I suppose that every father with female children probably goes through the same worries, that the young punk taking his child out is a sex-crazed maniac intent on the things that teenage boys are intent on. Somewhere in the preceding years, perhaps at the moment of birth of our girl-child, all of us dads have morphed from that punk into a responsible parent. If we are lucky, we recall our own past behaviors, and remember both the difficulty of being a teenager and the dangers inherent in two teenage humans of the opposite sex being left alone.

It requires a delicate balance to allow the child to explore life and to protect them from the wild world out there. Somewhere in between locking them up in the basement and giving them the car keys and the VISA card, sits the reasonable middle ground. It is my job—every parent's job, in fact—to find that middle ground. And that is the hard part. I hope that I will have the wisdom and maturity to know when to let go, when to hold on, and when to trust luck. For the moment, I am glad that the real big terrors—the first solo drive, the first date, the first night she doesn't come home—are still a ways off. But they are just over the horizon.

My little girl is eight. In a brief five years, the magical age of thirteen will descend upon her, with all of the wonders of moving from child to teenager. Puberty will be with us. I remember being a thirteen-year-old male, realizing that all the girls were changing. And that I liked the change. It is easy to become frightened of what may happen, given rising rates of teen pregnancies, the looming threat of AIDS, and who knows what other horrors.

So I gird myself for the day when my children will need to have sex explained. I practice the approach that I will take—not too forceful, not too lackadaisical. It must make sense, not scare them, and emphasize the point that sex should have a lot to do with love. Somehow, my wife and I have to give them enough information to allow them to make an intelligent decision, and we will hope that we have raised them right. And if not, then I'll scare the hell out of my daughter's dates.

Which is why I'm considering a subscription to *Guns and Ammo,* to start getting a feel for the right sort of weapon to have. Most of my peers express a similar concern. They aren't any more keen on hand guns than I am, but as our daughters creep toward the teen years, the virtues of gun ownership become clearer. Of course, my view is that of the father toward his little girl. Whatever explanation Freud may offer, fathers are naturally protective of their daughters. Sons, on the other hand, are supposed to require less care, and to be within the domain of their mothers.

My wife reassures me that I am overreacting, as usual. Marie isn't at all worried about the female child. She will be raised with good sense and a strong will (I can believe that), and she will know just how to deal with boys. No, Marie doesn't dread the day Sarah goes out on her first date. She lives in fear of the day when Max comes home in a state of rapture with his new love, a cocktail waitress named Loretta, snapping her gum as she says, "Pleased ta meetcha."

Uncle Ben

My family's home is Texas. Specifically a small, quiet city, just north of Dallas, called Farmer's Branch. I spent three or four summers of my childhood in Farmer's Branch, in the little white house where my mother grew up, with its Bermuda grass lawn and goldfish pond. It was a bit like visiting an alien world, where people spoke with a slow, easy accent. This was not the stereotype red-neck shit-kicker drawl, but a rich, wide, and warm way of speaking that sometimes made me wish I spoke that way.

In the odds and ends of experiences I have inherited from my mother, one phrase seems to be unique to my family. Certainly it could have come only from the South: "I swear to brown dog." My mother's uncle used this phrase with real conviction—some days when he was truly and passionately upset, he'd stand out in the barnyard and swear a blue streak at the old brown Labrador until he felt better.

My brother and I spent hot, lazy afternoons under the shade trees at the house in Farmer's Branch, visiting my grandmother and Aunt Ola, playing with second and third cousins, and swimming in any of the number of local pools. It was an adventure of sorts, getting to know a different side of my mother and her family, listening to long and complex explanations of family connections, which cousin was related to me through which aunt or grandparent. Of great interest was the story of my distant ancestor, Noah Good, who had come to Texas in 1846 to settle in Peter's Colony in Dallas County. In a nearby housing development, a well Noah had dug with his own hands and encased in a rough stone wall sat unused in a green belt between the streets. To this day, the well is called Noah's Well by the locals.

In Seattle, we didn't have any family around but ourselves, and that bred a stark and lonely feeling at times. In Texas, the constant stream of distant and not-so-distant cousins, great-aunts, and uncles was awe-inspiring to a boy who claimed only a father, mother, brother, and sister for family. Most of my grandmother's kin lived in and around Edna, a small town south of Farmer's Branch. My great-uncle Carver was the town barber, my great-uncle Ben raised cows and owned a meat packing plant just outside of town. Neither of my parents had siblings, so my great-aunts and uncles were the next best thing, and Uncle Ben was A-number one in my book.

I loved Ben. He drove a big Ford pickup with a tool box in the back, and when we cruised through Edna, he made me feel like we had been buddies all of my life, even though we had spent hardly any time together at all.

Ben took me to my first cattle auction and taught me the subtle art of bidding for half-ton steers. Each bidder had his own way of communicating silently with the auctioneer, making offers and counters with a toss of the head, a twitch of the eye. I sat fidgeting and squirming the way small boys will, until Ben leaned over and said, "You best sit still, boy. Your dancing around just raised the price on that cow five hundred dollars!" I was terrified, wondering how I could have done that and where was I going to get the money, until Ben looked at me and smiled, and I knew in an instant that I had been had.

One afternoon, Ben and I drove out to the pastures to select a cow for slaughter, and the next day he had a family barbeque for all the relations. I remember the trip to the meat processing plant, and my realization that we had picked out a quiet, brown-eyed animal to be killed and cleaned and cut up into pieces. It upset me, especially the smell that hung around the plant.

Very gently, Ben sat me down, and carefully and calmly explained the butchering process to me. He allowed as how the thought of doing in animals that he raised and cared for wasn't always a pleasant one. But that was the way the world worked. Animals were for eating, just like plants and fish and milk and eggs. And, if I was really upset about it, he was sorry and he hoped I'd still be his friend.

Well, of course I was still Ben's friend; in fact, that conversation sealed my love and loyalty for him. When he died a few years later, a part of my childhood was amputated by the thought that I would never see him again. I had not spent enough time with him to begin with.

I made my last family visit to Texas in 1980. I saw all of the surviving members of the clan, grown up and changed. The little white house is gone now, torn down to make way for a freeway on-ramp or a mall, and much of the family has scattered to the four winds. The older folk still live in Edna, a few in nearby Richardson and Carrolton. Every year my grandmother reports on the constant cycle of death and marriage and birth.

Texas is as much a state of being and emotion as anything else. It is big and wild and is as different from Washington as fire from rain. On occasion in my travels, I meet someone from Texas, and I gladly volunteer that I am a Texan, by blood if not upbringing, and we talk about Dallas and Houston and Lubbock, and a small city called Farmer's Branch.

Not that I really think of myself as a Southerner or a Texan. Perhaps I am becoming nostalgic in my middle years for a place that has the solid feel of home. I can't say as I can explain it, but it feels right. Perhaps it is the realization that I have a family.

The home that I am most comfortable with is the Northwest, where I was born and raised. The flatlands around Dallas, the dry hills of Fredricksburg, and the dune country out by Odessa are the antithesis of the mountains and rain and great stretches of fir and pine that are Washington. But every so often, I catch someone bad-mouthing Texas, making fun of Southerners, and the hair stands up on the back of my neck and my tone gets tight, and I swear to brown dog, long and loud.

Fur Balls and Fleabags

Now that they are old enough to have some rational thoughts, both of my children have begun dropping less-than-subtle hints about what sort of pets they'd like to have. Never mind that we have two cats already, neither of whom are of much use unless you count the fact that they eat those totally disgusting hockey pucks of processed animal parts described with such delicious names as Savory Stew and Beef Delight.

There isn't anything extraordinary about our family pets. Our cats are pretty run of the mill: an old, senile, scowling lady cat named Nigel Morningstar, and Winston Churchill, our yellow tabby, former tom and resident village idiot. Average, everyday, ho-hum cats.

I have been told that having pets helps reduce stress, resulting in a longer life, greater happiness, clearer skin, and economic prosperity. I must respectfully disagree. Our cats contribute to my lack of sleep, financial ruin, and frequently, near-mortal injuries, as I chase them around the house when the pair of them insist on playing hockey in the living room at 2 AM.

Soon after play begins my wife jabs her elbow in my ribs, indicating I am required to wake up, and head out on a search-and-seizure for one or both of the cats. This means teetering and staggering down the stairs without benefit of light or glasses, and then playing chase with the cats until I finally corner them and throw them outside. As you will no doubt have guessed, this is not my favorite thing in the world to do, not by a long stretch. It does not make me predisposed to adding animals to the household.

Winston, the newest member of our family, may also be the first to go if he doesn't learn to straighten up and fly right. His vet bills alone are justification for dismissal. A few months ago, he decided to tangle with a dog, who in turn tried to bite him in half. Winston subsequently disappeared for three days. As it turned out, the whole time we searched for him, he was doing a Siegfried-quality death scene under the deck. When we finally did find him, I had to peel up half of the deck to get him out in one piece. During this procedure, Winston protested my efforts, mewling, "Really, it's okay, leave me here to die . . . I'm a goner . . . don't trouble yourself, really. . . ."

Winston didn't die, thanks to the wonders of veterinary medicine—a two hundred dollar wonder to be precise. He was cleaned up and injected and given a nifty haircut—they shaved his entire side and back to get to the wounds. He ended up fine. I, however, not only had to pay his bills but also force-feed him antibiotics and clean the wound. All of which was relatively disgusting. That being that, we let life get back to normal.

Winston, however, wasn't content with this state of affairs. My theory is that he actually enjoyed the extra attention during his recovery. Once healed, he soon decided to play chicken with a very large auto. Bloodied but unbowed, he again disappeared under the deck to quietly contemplate his fate. For three days Marie and I stood outside and hollered. We tried tempting him with the offer of an entire Chinook salmon for breakfast. Winston, in his misery, refused to give out so much as a whimper or meow; not one small clue as to his whereabouts was forthcoming.

On a hunch, we peeled the deck up again, and once we discovered his deathbed, we dragged him off to see the animal doctor. The vet explained that this time Winston had snapped his tail, broken his pelvis in half, and skinned his toes. Our options were plain and simple: to let nature take its course, which meant that he'd probably be crippled for the rest of his life, or have his injuries surgically remedied. Four hundred dollars later, Winston was tailless, and had two stainless steel pins holding his nether regions together. Not to mention another nifty haircut. This time they shaved his entire back end except for his legs, so he looked a little like a poodle.

At this point I sat Winston down and patiently explained to him that he had used up all his credit with me. No more trips to the vet in 1995. And I would feel perfectly justified in laughing at him as he waddled around the house with his shaved backside. For two months after that, whenever he heard me come up behind him, he turned around and quickly sat down, as if to cover the indignity of his bald butt. Personally, I liked having him shaved—the big white spot made him a lot easier to find in the middle of the night.

So when my wife and children raise the subject of more pets, I am quite reasonably skeptical. I don't want to talk about puppies and dogs. Puppies have two purposes in life: to pee on the carpet and chew on everything and everyone handy. Plus all of the *really* good dogs already belong to other people, which is great as far as I am concerned. That way, I get to visit them without having any of the responsibility. Sort of like being the noncustodial parent in a divorce.

The dog issue being one on which I refuse to bend, the subject has turned to goldfish, hamsters, gerbils, and guinea pigs. Especially guinea pigs. In Sarah's class at school, they have a guinea pig named Fluffy, although I think Fluffo is a more appropriate for the fat little ball of fur. Sarah's teacher says that one of her favorite things to do is to sit with Fluffy in her lap and hand-feed the critter apple slices and lettuce from her lunch (instead of eating them herself). Sarah is absolutely in love with the idea of getting her own pet guinea pig, and when we stop in the pet store, she hovers longingly over the furry animal pens, watching all the rodents play and eat and make little pellets of fertilizer.

I suppose if we did get a guinea pig, in a pinch we could always eat it. In South America, the filleted varmints are plastic-wrapped and sold with the chicken breasts. After all, one man's pet is another man's hors d'oeuvres. But I haven't the heart to tell Sarah that in some parts of the world (most notably New Guinea) Fluffy would be considered a delicacy—smothered, baked guinea pig is apparently quite popular.

Max seems to have this very idea in mind. Instead of a dog or a rat, Max has asked quite earnestly, if we could get a cow as a pet. It would be a little cow, he explained, so it wouldn't take up too much space, and it could live in his room, and he could get milk for his morning cereal that way. But, Max, we replied, we have kitties, and the cow might step on them. Maybe we should discuss this after we don't have kitties anymore. Max thought on this for a moment and brightly suggested that we could "die" the kitties, and then the cow wouldn't step on them.

I can see the positive aspects of Max's idea. If the cow got whacked by a car and crawled under the deck, it'd be pretty easy to find it. And if the injuries were truly serious, well, I like ground beef and steak just fine.

Year of the
Bear

June had come, and I was free. I ran from Seward Elementary with my Scooby Doo lunch pail, a torn and dirty sweatshirt streaming behind me Batman-fashion, held to my head by the hood. I charged up the hill and darted across the street against the light, dogged by the shouts of the crossing guard.

No recess, no Pledge of Allegiance, no arguments while choosing up sides for kickball and red rover. Soon my dad would pack up the Rambler station wagon, the white one he kept threatening to paint a bright-red racing stripe down the middle of. Secretly, I wished he would.

He packed the Rambler with the old canvas tent, the white gas stove, tools, sleeping bags—all the camping gear we have—stuffed in, tied on, and somehow made to fit around the four of us: dad, mom, my older brother, and me. My dad never traveled light. He always packed as though we were going to South

America. The bare minimum included hand tools, saws, hammers, nails, chisels, chain saw, paint, tarps, chairs—everything that we might possibly need for the upcoming weeks in the wilderness.

This was the routine every summer of my childhood—before the firestorm of my parents' divorce, and the end of family trips. The four of us drove east from Seattle, across the Cascade Mountains to eastern Washington, through Spokane, and north into Pend Orielle Country and to the foothills of the Canadian Rockies. In between Kaslo and Castlegar is Kootenay Lake.

At the north end of the lake, the small Quaker community of Argenta sits above Johnson's Landing. Here we stripped the Rambler of its load and repacked the gear, this time into a boat. In went the comic books, *Spiderman* and the *Fantastic Four*, acquired in Nelson with Canadian Monopoly money, the Cadbury chocolate bars, the Rice Krispies labeled in French and English, plus a few days' worth of fresh food bought at the last possible moment before we pushed off and left. A small tinfoil package was added after a brief stop in Argenta. My mom and dad visit with their old friends, the Wolfes, and Mrs. Wolfe, Ruth, sent along a package of the best cookies ever made, carefully wrapped in the foil.

The moment we pushed away from the dock signaled a step away from the home behaviors my parents have so carefully drilled into my brother and me. My mother remembers how we turned into something wild: skin roasted nut brown and hair nearly bleached white by the summer sun, scabbed here and there from mosquito bites scratched too many times. We lived most summers in bathing trunks or shorts, and only wore shoes when we hiked in the woods.

On the far shore, a point of land marks where Fry creek snakes down through the woods from the falls. Several dozen people from various churches around the northwest arrived here throughout the summer to swim, play, visit, and catch up on the past year. We set up camp on a sandy knoll, just short of the trees. This was *our* spot, with a view of the water and mountains. It always felt right.

There were no roads here, no water except what came from the creek or the lake, no toilets beyond the pits that were dug every year. Evenings were illuminated by the hissing glow of the Coleman lamp, and the band of the Milky Way was a conspicuous halo of light, easily seen while standing on the beach. I can hardly distinguish among the summers that I spent there, the endless hours of capture the flag, swimming, and hiking to the pools at the base of the falls to fish for trout.

But one summer does stand out. One summer when it was especially hot, the camp trash pit became too big and too ripe amidst the press of people and the heat of the day. "We really need to do something about the pit," my father would occasionally remark, over a morning cup of tea. "Really got to do something."

And then the bears came. We heard them at night, rooting through the abandoned jelly jars and paper plates, snuffling and fighting over a few scraps. The adults warned us where to play and when, and to run from the bears if we saw them—the worst advice you can give about bears. I don't know why they told us to do that. Perhaps they knew it was what we would do regardless of what they said.

One afternoon, a bunch of menfolk went off toward the trash pit with a jerry can of gasoline and the flare pistol from the boat. My mother urgently shooed us out of camp, down the hill to the lake, to swim. Just as we had changed into our trunks, there was a muffled boom off in the woods, and a few minutes later, small charred bits of paper began to rain gently onto the camp.

That night the bears came back anyway, except this time they raided the camp itself, ransacking coolers. The next morning we found bags of flour and half-eaten apples spread through the ruin of the camp kitchen.

The men held a "serious" meeting that evening. They stood around looking stern, with issues to weigh, smoking pipes and cigarettes, and muttering. Children were sent off to bed, away from the doings, sure that something terrible was about to happen. The next morning, two or three of the men went across the lake in the boat, returning a few hours later with Bob Orr, a local hunter. He had on camouflage, and was carrying several rifles.

We were all abuzz with this. Guns! There were never any guns in camp—they were bad, we had been told, meant to kill people.

That night, after dinner, Bob and some of the men set out into the woods, armed with the rifles and flashlights. My brother and I lay awake in our sleeping bags for a while, listening as they crashed around in the dark, shouting at each other. Something was about to happen, and the excitement made me twist and turn, uncomfortable and anxious. After a bit, rain started to drum on the roof of our tent, and I fell asleep.

The next morning, the bear's hide—the symbol of the night's success—was stretched out, bloody side up, pegged to a bed of pine needles a little way from our camp. The flies hovered and buzzed over the mess. Someone had cut off the paws, and the body lay in a great, horrible, bloody mass to one side, its stench building in the morning sun.

We stood around it, staring at the bear's body like gawkers at an accident. What was this awful thing and why didn't somebody take it away? The boys dared each other to touch it, but none would. The adults argued whether they should butcher it, or get rid of it. In the end, the carcass was quickly dumped in a deep pit in the woods.

For several years afterwards, discovering the exact resting place of the bear was of keen interest to my brother and me. Somewhere in among the trees, the spirit of the animal hid, and we picked several different clearings that seemed right as animal graveyards. These became favorite places to hide from the adults in the evening, to tell scary stories until our spines tingled with a delicious mix of fear and excitement.

A child's world contains many fears. I feared being lost, abandoned and alone, disappointing my mother or father, being disliked and unloved. In the adult years that have come and gone since the death of the bear, I have come to understand that the pact between child and parent is one of love and protection: I love you, and I will allow no harm to befall you. I love you, and I understand that you will protect me. When the monster that lives in the shadows begins to move and bump, I will call out for you to save me, and you will rush into my room, hold me to your chest, and tell me that it is okay, you are here. Yet, somewhere inside themselves, children understand that the monster really isn't all that bad. The worst the monster does is inspire fear, and the fear is conquered with love.

The death of the bear, the mutilated and bloody corpse,

frightened me much more than the thought of its running wild. There was never a rational explanation. It happened, was done and over and never spoken of again. The murder of the monster, the poor, misunderstood beast, somehow diminished the protector, and my faith was shaken. Killing the bear, skinning it, and dumping it in a hole did not seem like the act of the protector.

I returned to Kootenay in 1980. The year of the bear had slipped from my mind. I set up camp on the same sandy knoll and watched the stars come out that night. The next morning, I walked the old trail to the falls. As I climbed deeper into the woods, I began to remember. I stopped and stood still in the patchy shade of the Douglas fir, and the only sound was the creek a few yards off. So many years after the killing, the lake seemed very much the same. The stand of trees was still there, a bit taller, and the creek still ran cold and swift. The spirit of the bear still seemed to be there in the woods, and since that day, I find that I cannot return.

Bonding

I can actually remember when it was quite a long ways left of center for a man to wear an earring. Back in the 1970s, when I was a teenager, I worked up the courage to have one ear pierced. I ended up with a simple gold stud in my ear. Some of my friends thought I was pretty daring, others thought I was nuts, more than one thought I was advertising my sexuality. At the time, I felt like I had taken a huge leap in defining myself by my gumption in wearing an article of jewelry, regardless of what any one thought.

Today, an earring—even two—in a man's ear is no big deal. I know engineers and stockbrokers who wear earrings. Now you know when an engineer does it, it has to be passé. And there is a whole herd of six- and seven-year-old boys running around my neighborhood sporting pint-sized zircon studs in their ears the way my buddies and I used to wear crew cuts and black canvas hightops.

The trend seems to be toward extreme, more flamboy-ant, methods of self-expression through bodily modification. Dull, everyday, the simple earring is now just a stage passed through on the way to more fashionable mutilation. Tattoos have been added to the acceptable forms of decoration for middle-American teens. Not that this is anything all that new. After all, guys of our father's generation have had SEMPER FI and USMC tat-toos ever since they served a tour of duty in the Korean War. And, by contrast to piercing of the body (and I don't mean ears), tattoos seem pretty tame.

There is a shop in Seattle that sells all sorts of hip and cool stuff, from housewares and linens, right through to clothing and jewelry. All the people who work there are perfect models for the store's merchandise, mid-twenties and in step with the cur-rent style rage.

For reasons still unclear to me, I found myself there one day buying some cool doo-dad totally inappropriate for my life-style. The brief encounter I had at the register made me realize just what lengths people will go to be fashionable. The woman tending the register had about five earrings in each ear, as well as one each in her nostril and eyebrow. And, exposed by the truncated T-shirt she wore, her belly button sported a little gold hoop, with a small bell that softly tinkled as she moved to ring up my purchase.

None of these things are truly foreign or strange to me. Sure, it was verging on extreme, but I've seen stuff like that before, and I carried on polite banter with her about the weather, and other inane stuff. As we chatted, I noticed that she spoke with a slight lisp, and as I looked at her, I found its source. Every time she opened her mouth to speak, I caught a glimpse of the pin she was wearing through her tongue.

I do not want to think about what sort of nerve or alcoholic stupor it took to have that done. I cannot imagine why she did it either, but that seemed to be the extent of her self-imposed piercings. That I could see. Who knows what other parts of her flesh she might have shoved steel and gold pins through. I shudder to think about that.

My daughter Sarah has been toying with the idea of having her ears pierced for about a year. Her mother told her that whenever she was ready (in other words when she had worked up the courage) it was just fine for her to have it done. The message was that it was to be *her* choice. But Sarah's skittish nature held her in check, wanting very much to do it, being very frightened that it would hurt like the dickens.

One Saturday afternoon, as Sarah and her mother and I were strolling through the mall, Sarah asked out of the blue if we thought that anyone would be getting their ears pierced today. We said we didn't know, but we could go see. As it turned out, three young women, all sisters, ranging from about ten to fifteen, were having their ears done all at the same time, each encouraging the others. Sarah watched, and fidgeted a lot, unable to work up the courage. Her mother, in a flash of brilliance, looked at her and said, "It doesn't hurt. Your daddy had his ear pierced when I first met him." Then she looked at me, and said with a smile that telegraphed her thoughts to me, "You should get it repierced."

I can take a hint as well as the next guy. I asked Sarah if she wanted to get her ears done, and was she scared. She answered yes to both. I suggested that I could get my ear repierced, too, I could go first, and would that help, to see me have it done, too?

Ten minutes later, I was standing next to my daughter, feeling the slight burning tingle in my ear lobe, and watching Sarah steel herself for the moment. Two people from the shop were enlisted to help, to fire both pins through her ears at the same time, and Sarah hunched and scrunched down into a tiny ball as the guns were attached to her ear lobes. "Honey, " I said, "closing your eyes isn't going to make any difference."

One, two, three, pop, and she opened her mouth and eyes as wide as she could, claiming that it didn't hurt. She talked about it for three days afterward, talking enthusiastically about how easy it was. With the snap of the pin in the piercing gun, a big part of her fear had just ceased to exist.

From my perspective, I can take or leave an earring, and I don't particularly care if Sarah wears earrings. It doesn't really matter to me. The only downside, if there is one, is that people I work with give me a pretty bad time about it. Not that I care. If my getting up into the chair first helped Sarah do it too, well then it was worth it. There are a number of ways that a father and daughter may bond together, from camping and activities of all sorts, through just sharing interests. The piercing of body parts would not have been high upon my list, but I am a firm believer that you take life as you find it.

I love my daughter, I enjoy sharing things with her, but there is a limit. I'll tell you right here and now, matching tattoos are out of the question. And, while I was "bold" enough to get my ear pierced way back when, if she wants to get her tongue pierced, she is on her own.

On the Joys of Giving

I have always considered myself creative. But I'm afflicted by a strange malady—the "Pre-Birthday Brain Lock Syndrome." I tend to freeze up about two months before any given birthday, and try as I might, I just cannot come up with good gift ideas without something close to a life and death struggle.

This condition is intensified when it comes time to buy gifts for my father. He has always been hard to pick gifts for. Part of the reason for this is that when he sees something he likes, he buys it. He appreciates certain standard fallbacks, but you can only buy chocolate, cigars, and cognac so many times before they get to be old hat. The other problem is that my father is an extremely imaginative man. He's already thought of a lot of the more unique ideas I come up with.

A couple of years ago, I decided to give up buying my father things, and began to give him *experiences* instead.

One memorable year, I arranged for us to use the Boeing 767 flight simulator in Seattle for a couple of hours. We were able to practice approaches to Boeing field to our heart's content. And we also managed to land safely, if you stretch the definition of "safely" to include parking the airplane in the Duwamish waterway.

Less successful was my gift of a weekend in an underwater research station in the Florida Keys that had been converted to a bed-and-breakfast inn. Unfortunately, relishing that experience required a valid scuba diving certificate, and since my father doesn't like to dive, the idea was scratched.

Never mind. The very best gift so far was the crane ride. Now I don't mean some little wimp of a crane. I mean one planted over a major skyscraper under construction, at least thirty stories above the pavement, swinging massive steel beams around like balsa wood. A real, working crane. A manly crane.

You see, my father has always wondered how cranes work. And, as I am the one in the family with the scientific bent, I had been asked several times over the years to set him straight on why cranes don't just fall over. I tried explaining about the physics of it all, counterbalances, moments of inertia and torque. He told me that was all nonsense: it was clearly *magic* that held them up. His resistance to the facts sounded like a golden gift opportunity.

I know some people in the construction business, and made a few phone calls trying to find someone who had an active construction site with a *real* crane. And a well-developed sense of adventure. I mean, the liability of letting a man in his late middle age climb up the innards of heavy machinery anchored to the ground far below is a serious issue.

As it happens, I was able to find a company that was involved in the steel work on a new skyscraper in downtown Seattle. I called the job foreman and explained my request. He listened politely to my proposal, thought a moment, and agreed to let us climb the crane—if we would sign a waiver exonerating his company from blame should we happen to die, be maimed, or fall through the roof of a passing bus. So I made up a gift certificate, to be delivered on my father's birthday, complete with a photo of the crane.

My father, for all of his easy nature, is a very controlled man, and it is rare to see him really bust loose. But that birthday, after he opened the envelope, he stomped his feet and laughed and asked three times if it was a *real* crane. It was just the sort of thing that he hadn't ever thought to arrange for himself but had always wanted to experience.

Perfect.

The day for the crane ride was a normal Seattle day—cloudy, windy, and very wet. My father and I (hey, I wouldn't miss it) donned gloves, rain slickers, and bright orange hard hats, signed the required papers, and then placed ourselves in the care of the site foremen.

We rode to the top floor of the building in a construction elevator, and then climbed onto an open ladder inside the crane, two or three hundred feet up. All the way up, I kept thinking that perhaps I had overestimated the quality of the gift, in contrast to the possibility of slipping and falling out of the crane tower. It was a very, very long way down, and my palms were sweating long before we actually made it to the top. I was scared as all hell.

The climb was worth it. The cloud ceiling was just above the

Columbia Center, and the view, even on this rainy day, was spectacular. The crane operator kept on working, so we were treated to the sight of several very large steel I beams being plucked off waiting flatbed trucks and swung into precise locations on the building.

We spent an hour or so watching the work and about twenty minutes talking to the operator about what he did, and most important, why the crane didn't topple over. The operator explained about counterweights, moments of inertia, torque, admitting at last that the crane just sort of leans back from the load, enough so that it doesn't fall over. Most of the time. None of this held any sway with my father, who still insisted that it was magic.

But I felt, at least this time, that I had made the magic real.

The Lies I Tell

One morning in the middle of May, on the drive to school, Max was deep in thought, unusually quiet since the moment we pulled out of our driveway. His sister had been singing and laughing, but Max's brow was furrowed as he wrestled with some tough question.

"Daddy," he finally asked, "is Santa Claus true?"

Is Santa Claus true? What he means is, is Santa real, does he exist? Max, on this particular spring day, as the trees were filling out with leaves and the flowers were coming up, had decided that he doubted his belief in the white-bearded one. Why this question arises now, on a warm morning in May, is anyone's guess. The issue is that he needs to know, he needs reassurance. And he needs to know *now*.

Max's question hung there for a moment, unanswered. What do I tell my child, age five, and his eight-year-old sister? What is the "right" answer (not to be confused with the truth)?

"No, kids, I've been lying to you all of your lives. Santa is a figment of your collective imagination." That doesn't work too well. Or I could affirm the existence, this time, and let them go on in their belief for another year or two. Or I could just ignore the question, distracting Max by pointing out the really humongous garbage truck that was snorting and thrumming its way at us from the other direction.

Which is what I tried. Weighty philosophical questions such as the existence of Santa Claus and Good and Evil are best not addressed at seven in the morning, especially before I've had a cup of coffee.

But as children go, Max has the character of a bulldog. He is tenacious when I'd rather he wasn't, and he was not put off easily this morning. Ignoring the garbage truck, he repeated his question a little more firmly this time. An answer was demanded. So I pulled out my next level of defensive tactics. "Max, what do you think? Is Santa true?" That usually works—throw the query back at him, let him define his own values and beliefs. Isn't that part of being a good father, to help the child learn to make up his own mind?

Maybe under most circumstances, but not today. "I dunno," says Max.

"Ask Sarah then. She knows about Santa." The next dodge, pawn the question off onto his sister. If she believes, he will too.

But Sarah is looking out the window counting fire hydrants ("three red, seventeen yellow . . .") and doesn't feel like being cooperative this morning. She just shrugs when her brother asks ("four red, seventeen yellow . . ."). And the ball came straight back to me, aimed right at my head.

"Dad, IS SANTA TRUE?"

Faced with this situation, without my wife for backup, I

asked for a pause so I could think, could consider all the possible answers and their consequences.

Most of the kids who are the same age as my own believe in the mythical characters of our holidays, Santa and the Easter Bunny, and others like the Tooth Fairy. There is an early period in their lives when we, their parents, nurture these beliefs, and all of them get excited about finding a chocolate bunny hiding in a basket of fake grass, or a dollar under the pillow where a tooth had been. By some unspoken agreement, no parent will take the responsibility to disabuse them of the notions that these characters exist. It is a conspiracy of silence.

At some point, someone spills the beans. One child becomes infected with the truth. Like a bad case of flu or a head cold, the truth spreads through an entire class or group of children, and all the parents are obliged to come clean, to explain ourselves to our children. Still we find ways to soften the blow. "Yes, Santa is imaginary, but he stands for the love that we feel for each other." A fairly lame explanation, if you ask me, but the best we can do under the circumstances.

When one of the mythical creatures is revealed to be mom and dad, the whole group are found out. It's as though all of them are keystones in the arch that supports childhood's fantasies. Pull one of them out, any one of them, and the whole thing comes down. All the imaginary beings, all the characters from the bedtime stories come crashing down together, and the child takes a step toward growing up.

I remember when I stopped believing in Santa and the Easter Bunny, the elves and the Tooth Fairy. My brother and I were disabused of the fantasy the same year; he explained the truth to me, and I knew he must be right. Like most children, I wasn't really too upset about the it. After all, just because you stop believing in Santa doesn't mean you stop celebrating Christmas (or getting presents). And you've got to run out of teeth to hide under the pillow at some point, so the Tooth Fairy has a limited life span with any child. The children don't even get mad at those of us who have been lying to them. It's almost part of the tradition, a multigenerational lie. My parents lied to me about it because their parents lied to them about it, so it's okay if I lie about it, too. Max would one day no doubt lie to his own offspring about it.

I realized that ultimately, the right answer to Max's question is a resounding "sort of." True, there is no fat, bearded elf stuffing stockings with candy and toys. Instead, there is a pudgy, bearded father. I ate the cookies and drank the eggnog. And I took the carrots for the reindeer, sealed them in a Ziploc plastic bag, and put them in my lunch. The Tooth Fairy and the Easter Bunny are both named Mom. And the reason we act the parts is because we love our children, and we know that it is okay for them to believe fairy tales, for a while at least.

"Daddy, IS SANTA TRUE?"

Can it wait, for now, or do I go ahead and tell him? Do I deal with it now, when the opportunity presents itself, or do I wait for someone else to tell him? It is like the issue I will face with sex. It is better that I tell them than to let someone, possibly a kid, fill them with ideas that may have no grounding in the truth. I thought a moment, and did the only reasonable thing a father can do, when unreasonable pressure is brought to bear.

"Max, this is a very good question. Ask your mother."

Skate King

They are all gone. All of the vestiges of my childhood memories of birthday parties have been bulldozed to make way
for office parks or minimalls. No more can I have a pig trough
at Farrel's, Shakey's Pizza is a fading memory, and drive-in
movies are something I have to drive to Auburn to see. The last
bowling alley in my neighborhood is now a bookstore. All of
them are long gone. All except one.

In a quiet and moderately rundown neck of the woods, I was
pleasantly surprised to see that at least one small part of my
childhood lives on. Skate King, the last roller rink on this side of
the lake, is still there, nestled in the back of Evan's Plaza, behind
Baskin Robbins and a realtor's offices.

When I saw the rink's cinderblock flank peeking around its
neighbors, it stirred a small portion of my brain to connect a
few dusty synapses together, and memories suddenly bubbled

up. Overwhelmingly they said, and I quote, "*Damn!* That was *fun!*" As cliché as it may seem, a wave of nostalgia hit, and I was immediately in love with the idea of taking my family there, to do one of those "Look kids, this is what your daddy did before we had Nintendo" kind of memory trips.

I wasn't disappointed. The rink has survived, and in essence is the same place it was when I last visited, back in 1977. Though the style of music has passed from Disco and KC and the Sunshine Band to Rap and Nirvana, the beat is still there; you can dance to it. True, more people wear in-line "blade" skates now, and wide-collared satin shirts and frizzy perms have been replaced by Chicago Bulls T-shirts and baseball caps (worn backwards, of course).

But the essence is the same.

In fact, most of the essence is the same because the decor hasn't changed in twenty years. The carpeted areas are worn, the facilities are ancient, and the whole place still smells a bit like the disinfectant they hose the skates down with after each rental. Duct tape, the universal repair tool, abounds, holding frayed ends of carpeting down and hinges on lockers up. The things that count—the sound system and the rink itself—are in good shape. Walk in and feel the *whompawhompa* beat, hear the chatter of teens, and the whir of plastic wheels on the rink floor, and suddenly you are thirteen again. The disco glitter balls still fill the room with teenage romance as couples skate together to some slow and musky tune, and muted red and blue lamps make pools of color for the young lovers to glide through for a few moments of *ahhhhhhh*.

The rink still has games, like Four Corners, which is a little like musical chairs, except a lot more people win. They still have the famous "reverse skate" during which you can have the delightful pleasure of skating in the wrong direction. It is a welcome relief to strain your tendons the other way for a bit.

To my total astonishment, I skate just as well now as I did twenty years ago. And that is badly at best. I totter along that narrow line between upright and flat-on-my-face-on-the-floor. The straight-aways are my favorite, the place where I can get up a good head of steam before I tackle the terror of the curves. As I skitter along, waving my arms in a frantic effort to maintain my balance and stave off disaster, seven-year-olds in knee pads race past me, coming close enough to nick my skates with theirs but managing not to actually floor me. But the unwritten rules of the rink still require those who can skate to steer clear (mostly) of those who cannot, and most spills are self-induced. Children and novices still creep around the rink in single file, clutching the walls or the hand of a parent or more competent friend. I can identify with that.

Somehow, the next day's pain of long dormant muscles and skinned knees nagging at me, telling me that I am too out of shape for this, didn't matter. It was just too much fun. There is a sense of freedom of movement, of traveling fast without the pounding of feet on pavement or the roar of a motor, no gas pedal to push, just the gentle rhythm of your own legs pushing and rocking side to side. Skating has a relaxed state of grace to it that even a clumsy skater like me can appreciate.

It is impressive that this lone survivor of the '70s birthday party scene can still draw a crowd, especially when competing with Discovery Zone–type indoor playgrounds. But Skate King still does a pretty good birthday business. And every Saturday and Sunday, the skaters come out in droves. Herds of pubescent girls and boys abound, along with chaperones, small children, parents, and a few throwbacks, like myself. The place is packed.

There must be some good reason for that. All I can come up with is that skating is fun, anyone can do it, and it really is a great family outing. There are few enough sports that can make that claim.

Oh, and did I mention that it was fun?

Skate King hasn't been completely untouched by the '90s. Video games and Terminator pinball machines line the wall in one section, and it isn't that uncommon to see someone skating with a cellular phone or pager on his belt.

The best part of revisiting Skate King was taking my family, and trying to teach my two children the basics of gravity and balance. It is a difficult concept to master, but they both are trying, and I expect a miracle any day now. After all, they are much smarter than their dad, and someday I'll need them to hold me up.

It's a Bird, It's a Plane

Being a mother. Now there is a tough job.

Never mind the joys of carrying a baby, gaining forty pounds, hemorrhoids, leaky nipples, and that stuff. And disregard for a moment the no doubt deliriously uncomfortable sensation of shoving the net equivalent of a ten-pound bag of billiard balls through one's birth canal. True, these are hard and difficult moments, but there isn't that much debate over how these things are accomplished. Babies either come out through the planned avenue, or they are removed à la Julius Caesar.

As far as I can figure, having the baby is the "easy" part. I suspect that more than a few women, including my wife, have probably just concluded that I am an idiot, which may well be true. But it seems to me that the process of making and delivering a baby is a fairly linear one. It starts here, progresses in more or less this manner, and is delivered thus. Once the child is presented, squalling, covered in gunk, looking a lot like it's been hit by a truck, well, then the trouble really begins.

See, everybody wants to tell the mother how she ought to go about being just that, the mother. Everybody has an opinion. Very few people approached me and told me how to be a father. I was left to flounder around on my own and figure it out. But mothers, well, they not only are told by friends and mothers and mother-in-laws how it ought to be done, but they've even got magazines, TV segments, and radio talk shows all about the *right* way to be mom.

If you knew my wife these days, you would know that this was a grave mistake. She is too much of her own mind to accept unsolicited advice, especially when you are coming at her with it, intent on shoving it down her throat. Marie's reaction to this is not unlike that of a hungry lioness to the trainer trying to hand feed her. You're apt to lose the hand in which you hold the advice. But eight years ago, she was not so sure. Motherhood was an unknown then.

Upon the delivery of Sarah, Marie's name was added to the intergalactic mailing list of "New Mommies Needing Advice." She began to receive this magazine, *Incredibly Successful and Talented Working Mommy,* the magazine for, well, incredibly successful and talented mommies who worked. It was full of very important advice and tips, like how to perform a leveraged buyout while breast-feeding, preparing your toddler for Yale, and the Paris designers' fall lines for PTA meetings.

The cover of this magazine was always essentially the same: some young and attractive woman posing with her equally attractive child. An article inside, the cover proclaimed, would tell you how this woman managed to run her own multimillion-dollar business, a business she started on her kitchen table, maintain a good marriage with a sensitive and caring husband, maintain her figure, cook gourmet meals, and still have time to paint, sculpt, write poetry, tune the BMW, and do volunteer work at the local homeless shelter. Staying at home with the child never crossed her mind.

Wow. What a woman, you'd think. Of course, the article never mentioned the fact that she had a live-in nanny, a maid, a personal trainer, was taking sedatives to sleep, and mainlining espresso in the morning just to jump-start her heart. That was beside the point. The real issue, or so Marie thought, was that women like this were being held up to her as the role model she should aspire to. It reminded me a lot of *Playboy*, where a "perfect" woman was held up as the ideal, never mind the benefit of professional photographer, lighting, airbrush, or silicone. And the way in which the perfect working mother model was presented to Marie, well, that was like taking the Miss October centerfold and throwing it in her face and suggesting that if she didn't look like that, she wasn't making the cut.

And for a while, Marie tried her darndest to do just that. She had already decided that she was going to be a working mother. As much as she loves her children, she also wanted a career. And since I also happened to want a career, this meant that a large percentage of our children's early years would be spent in the company of day-care providers. Marie agonized over her decision, doubted her quality as a parent.

There is a good buzzword for this state: the mommy-trap. I prefer to think of it as the Super Mom syndrome. The articles that Marie read all came back to the same basic idea. In order to have worth, you need to be the perfect mother, businessperson, and wife. Be it all, do it all, and be the best at it.

Marie is damn good at everything she does. In the time I've known her, she has gone from being a customer service representative to being the regional financial manager for a Fortune 500 company, gotten both her bachelor's and master's degrees (with GPAs to kill for, thank you very much), had two children, and managed to maintain a marriage with a man whose idea of helping to make the bed is getting out of it. True, she does not own her company—not yet, anyway—and she doesn't run the Boston Marathon every year, just for laughs. But she has done pretty well, if you ask me.

So this Super Mom trap was rather bothersome. Every month, Marie got reinforcement that no matter what she was doing, it wasn't good enough. Some other mommy was doing it better, faster, grander. Some other mommy was making millions while spending quality time with the kids.

Adding to the confusion, in recent years a radio psychologist has come on the scene, who among other things rails on the idea that you should wait ten years into your marriage to have children and then you should be there for the child. Stay home until the child goes to school, and then be there at the bus stop to drop them off and pick them up. This is a nice fantasy, especially when presented by a woman who writes books and does a three-hour radio show for a living. I'd like to see how she felt about it if she had a real job, like file clerk or shift manager at McDonald's.

Conflicting advice. Images seemingly calculated to make her feel as though she was doing it all wrong. Like I say, the birthing was the easy part.

After eight years as a mom, Marie has finally found her comfort point. She let the magazine subscription lapse, in spite of the pleas from their circulation department and offers of half off the newsstand price, a free telephone shaped like a baby bottle, and a video of *Motherhood's Greatest Bloopers*. She retuned her car radio presets and steadfastly refuses to listen to radio know-it-alls. Let 'em talk and pontificate all they want. She has decided for herself that she is a mother, doing the best she can. The children are smart and happy, and so is she. She may not have *it all,* but it's close enough.

Some nights, though, after Marie thinks I have gone to sleep, she creeps into the bedroom and tries to quietly strip down and get into her jammies without disturbing me. I've fooled her, though, and I crack my eyes ever so slightly and watch her. It's hard to tell, since I don't have my glasses on and I can't see too well in the darkness of the room. But I'd swear, underneath her work clothes, she has a red and blue body stocking on, with this big gold crest across her chest. With what looks like an "S" on it.

Ant Farm

As the parent of small children, I can tell you the whereabouts of almost any toy store in the city I live in. From the "WE B' TOYS" warehouses stocked with five million pounds of plastic, through the high-end FOB Swharzenhoople with the platinum-coated Legos, I know them all well. And, boy howdy, do they know and love me and my credit card every bit as much.

I've come home with some pretty remarkable things. Walking, talking, screaming and singing dolls, dolls that wet, robots that turn into trucks and planes. After a while, it all looks the same, and I've begun looking for better stuff. Maybe some toys that are *educational.*

Just recently, I discovered a great toy store that specializes in thought-provoking toys, toys designed to catch a child's interest in science and the world. They've got chemistry sets, games which teach world geography, rock polishers, gyroscopes, and science projects. All manner of gizmo and doo-dad, fun but with some learning aspect—like illuminating the greater world around us. Wandering through their aisles, I discovered the ultimate in live-action toys.

No, not live-action as in a toy that does some superhero stunt when you touch a button, but real "live" creatures, animals and insects that move through the grace of nature rather than a couple of AA batteries. There is one that is called a butterfly garden—you get a big mesh box with half a dozen caterpillars. In another, a jar of frog eggs, and in a third a box of earthworms. And there is the old standby, the Ant Farm. I bought them all.

I like the live-action stuff. The caterpillars made cocoons and changed from ugly, squidgy things into beautiful butterflies. The frog eggs became tadpoles and eventually real frogs, which tried to eat the butterflies at every turn. And the earthworms ate a whole bunch of garbage and made nice potting soil and lots more worms, teaching the children about recycling and the reproductive habits of worms. All pretty cool, and all lessons about nature and life.

Except the ants. All of the other critters did cool stuff. They grew and changed. But the ants just died.

There is something incredibly sad about the ant farm. Tragic, in fact.

At first, it was very exciting. We got a big plastic house for the ants, with clean, white sand, a little cut-out of a farm, a five-year supply of ant chow, and a coupon good for one ration of ants. We assembled the farm, and sent the coupon in, and then we waited. One day, a tube of ants arrived in the mail. The children and I excitedly put them into their new home (we held the tube over the hatch and shook it real hard), and gave them food and water. And then we settled in to watch them do what ants do, which is dig tunnels and move dirt. By the next morning, they had the beginnings of a pretty impressive tunnel system. Within a couple of days, they had reshaped their entire landscape, moving grains of sand here and there with some intense purpose in mind. We watched the whole time, fascinated.

And then the ants died. Not all at once, but one at a time, as though a plague was moving through them. One by one, the population diminished. This ant here, struggling up a hill with a boulder of quartz in her mandibles, suddenly felt a pain in her front left leg. She dropped the rock, and stopped to rest a moment. But moments later, she moved no more.

One by one, the corpses collected. The survivors, ever neat and tidy, gathered their honored dead in one spot, a common grave for the fallen. After two or three days, there were only a few left, then four or five, and then, within a week, only one. And in the end, she too succumbed, perhaps dying from the loneliness that a creature used to the company of the hive would find horrible. As the last, she left no offspring to mourn her passing, no future, no monument beyond the maze of tunnels dug into the clean white sand for no purpose beyond "because."

When our last ant bought the farm (so to speak), I wondered what sort of lesson my children had learned. What sort of toy is it that results in the wholesale death of an ecosystem? I know that they had seen the inner workings of the tunnels, watching the ants work and cart and tote and carry, and that was all very interesting.

Did they see this existence of working for no apparent purpose, inside the walls of a plastic prison, followed shortly by death? Did they feel the sadness, the ants destined to perform the same tasks, even with no queen to make new workers? Were they touched by this? Did they see the lesson?

Naw. They thought ants were cool. Too bad they all died. Could we order some more?

Follicularly
Challenged

M arie and I went out to our favorite Mexican restaurant the other night to celebrate our first date, which occurred on April 1, all of twelve years ago. We decided to take the kids with us, as sort of a reminder of where we've been and where we are going. We're both showing the signs of approaching middle age. A little thicker around the middle, a few more lines here and there. And we both have less hair than we did when on our first date. Marie has cut hers shorter, and I will never worry about matching my father's silvery gray, because I am losing my hair. Slowly, to be sure, but quite steadily.

Marie and I told the kids about the old days, the time before they came along, when we were both younger. Sarah listened thoughtfully through this, and then asked me if my hair was going to "go away." Was I going to go bald. I said yes, some of my hair was falling out, that I would certainly have less hair as I got older. She started to cry and said that she didn't want me to lose my hair. Why, I asked. Because I would look stupid, she said, and cried some more. I asked, does her papa (meaning her maternal grandfather, who went bald in his twenties) look stupid? No, came the response. So it's okay if daddy loses his hair, right? NO! Why? "Cause you'd look stupid. . . ."

I don't mind losing my hair. Its been slow so far, just the beginnings of moderate deforestation. My stepmother, the doctor, calls it "Male Pattern Baldness," which means that horseshoe shape the hairline begins to take. I don't know how far it will go, but I don't worry too much. I have a barometer for the future of my hair. I can look at my older brother, who is two years ahead of me in all things including hair loss. I don't worry too much, since he's still got most of his. Plus there is not a thing I can do about it.

My mother's father gave me his hair genes, and that's all there is to it. I hope to thin or go bald gracefully, never turning to a rug, and I have already vowed never to be one of those guys who grows the hair long on one side and combs it over the top. When I see one of those guys on a windy day, trailing their hair behind them like the tattered remnants of a flag, it's a sign of defeat. I think that trying to conceal your baldness is a bit foolish, like plucking eyebrows and then penciling them back in. What's the point?

When my son finally started getting some hair, I asked him why he even bothers. He got his hair from his grandpa, the guy who was losing it in a big way at age twenty-five. I tell Max that he's wasting his energy growing something that's going to fall out anyway. Perhaps he should concentrate on more productive tasks, like becoming the greatest quarterback in the history of professional football, complete with a lucrative contract so he can support me in the life-style to which I would like to become accustomed.

People have all sorts of bad associations with baldness. Age, lack of virility or strength, etcetera. I would like to point out that many great men were bald. Thomas Edison, for example, had thinning hair. Yul Brenner showed that a bald head could be masculine and virile. Napoleon was not only short but balding as well. And you could compile a list a mile long of famous and influential men who are or were going bald—Terry Bradshaw, Lyndon Johnson, the Duke of Wellington, Steve McQueen, Robert Oppenheimer, to name a few. An eclectic list to be sure, but bare pate has little to do with the man underneath, his intelligence or character.

Having a receding hairline does bring about a few life changes. You discover the virtues of wearing hats on cold days. You use sunscreen in new and exciting places. You spend less money on combs and other hair care products. You get discounts at the barber shop. The only real downside to baldness is if you happen to have an unattractive skull. I won't know for a while yet if I fall into that category, but I am keeping my fingers crossed. Perhaps I can fix any divots with a little Bondo and some flesh-colored spray paint.

Of course, just because the hair is thinning on one end of my skull doesn't mean I have to suppress it on the other end. I have always wanted to grow a beard. It is one of those rites of passage into manhood that I had secretly looked forward to. Boom! Puberty, hormones, thick and full facial hair—instant sex appeal (as well as that sophisticated look). But though I did manage to reach puberty, the beard-producing cells just didn't join in, not even to make a little stubble.

Now with traces of buffed pink scalp where once there was a mane, growing a beard to is much more imperative. It balances things out nicely. It exercises the follicles that survive. And it cuts down on the amount of time I have to spend shaving, which is an activity that I absolutely hate.

So I finally decided to order a beard from my less-than-furry face. I refused to shave, which was in itself a treat, and demanded action from the follicles. So as not to attract too much attention, I waited until I was on a two-week vacation. And by some miracle of modest proportions, growth occurred. Of course, my face looked terrible the whole trip, and it just looked a tad dirty by the time I got home. But now, many months later, the growth has finally come to resemble (vaguely) a beard.

Mind you, it isn't a real beard. I haven't the wherewithal to grow the General Burnside extravaganza or the biker dude from hell Mother of all Mustaches. Mine is one of those goatee-Van Dyke thingees. Just covers my upper lip and the ball of my chin. People tell me, though, that I would look like Jay Buhner, if he were shorter, fatter, and less well paid. Or that Jay Buhner would look like me if I could hit thirty homers in a season. I keep trying to get the verticals, from the mustache to the chin, to fill in, but they won't cooperate.

I'll never have a full beard, because I have one spot on my jawline that refuses to sprout anything at all. I'm follicularly challenged.

And the worst of it is seeing those guys in my office who can grow facial hair the way my lawn grows crab grass. These are the fellows with that permanent bluish tinge to their cheeks, the ones who have to shave from the top of their chest to the bottom of their jaw if they want to look well groomed.

And I hate 'em. I feel that there should be equal opportunity facial hair. Maybe even a government-sponsored program to facilitate the growth of proper beards. Maybe all of those women out there who have their upper lips depilated would donate their follicles to guys like me, who need a little help.

I'd really like to grow a full beard. I'd like to be able to wax the ends of my mustache and curl them up into neat little circles, pretend I'm an RAF fighter pilot, pip pip and eh what? I'd like to grow mutton chops, and a ZZ Top navel-length beard, and braid it. Just for the fun of it. And maybe ride a Harley-Davidson Shovel Head down Interstate 5, with my tresses streaming behind me, making horrible faces at passing tourists in Airstreams and Winnebagos—"Oh Henry, a man just went by on one of those hogs and he had on leather and a beard that was three feet long, and he looked like he was possessed by Satan himself, and I don't think we should stop in Washington."

But as with all things having to do with appearance, it is ultimately my wife's opinion that counts. She bought me a little pair of scissors and a matching comb and brush, just so I can cut the beard and mustache back to a reasonable length. To reinforce this, she will periodically pipe in with a "You need a trim."

So much for ZZ Top.

Coffee Milk
and Death

I like evenings, as the house quiets down and the children are mellowing out after the screaming-giggling-singing-jumping-up-and-down of the day's journey they have taken through school, learning and playing. The evening may end with watching television, or playing hide-and-seek—which is to say the children hide in the same places, and I pretend that I cannot find them. Some nights we play *Sorry!*, other nights we read books. Lately, as Sarah has begun to get comfortable with her reading skills, she likes me to listen to her read *Green Eggs and Ham* or *The Tale of Peter Rabbit.* It is nice to find a moment to just sit together after the rush of the day and the animated hullabaloo of dinner when everyone tries to tell everyone else what they did, all at the same time.

And some nights, we just sit and hang out together.

Sarah, Max, and I were sitting at the kitchen table one

evening, getting ready to call it a night. We were eating Oreos, twisting them open, licking and chewing the filling out, and then eating around the edge of each half in concentric circles until we had tiny bits of cookie left. I was once told by a nutritionist who worked for a diet center that it would take my body fifteen years to get rid of the fat I took in each time I had an Oreo. I'm not sure where she got that information—it sounds rather suspect to me. But true or not, at this stage of the game, I figure that by the time my body manages to get rid of all the fat, I'll have been dead for about six hundred years. In fact, when I go, they may want to claim the body to recycle the stuff. But no matter how bad they are supposed to be (and I insist they have no proof), I like Oreos. A lot.

To wash down the chocolate and frosting, Sarah had a big glass of milk, and the menfolk each have a cup of coffee milk— for Max, half milk, half decaffeinated coffee, a bit of sugar, and for me, a dollop of milk, some artificial sweetener (to help compensate for the Oreos), and a lot of decaf in a mug the size of small cat.

There was something wonderfully calming about sitting there with my children at the end of this day. Dinner was done, the dishes dumped into our electric scullery maid (the dishwasher), Sarah had finished a shower and was bundled up in her nightie (the Little Mermaid one), and Max was fresh from the bath, pink-cheeked and pretty cozy in his footie jammies. Every once in a while, they looked up from dissecting the cookies and caught me studying them. And they gave me the most amazing smiles, somewhere around completely cute with just a hint of impishness thrown in, just so I know that they aren't complete angels. I live for moments such as these.

The kids and I talk about all sorts of things at this time of night. What we did today, what they learned in school, what Max wants for his birthday (which is usually at least six months off when he mentions it), which kids Sarah is currently best friends with at school, and sometimes we even talk about what I did all day. They don't quite understand the tasks that an engineer has, but they at least pretend to be interested. Sometimes, though, the conversations get heavily involved in serious stuff.

My children have inquisitive minds that delve into a diverse group of subjects. They want to know all about science and electricity. They have a particular interest in what makes the world go. Sometimes we get into a very complex discussion about how something works or happened or what have you, and we have to go dig out the dictionary or a science book and see if we can uncover the truth of the matter.

Other times, though, Max and Sarah would prefer to wrestle with the deeper issues of life, the philosophical truths. "Daddy," Max asked this particular evening, "are you getting old?" Out of the blue, no warning.

I allowed as how I was always getting older. Somedays my back hurts more than others, now and then the knees crackle and pop ominously, and I notice that a few of the lines that appear on my face when I smile stay when I stop. I guess I am getting older. I asked what he meant by old.

"Your hands are old," he said, changing gears slightly as he grabbed my left thumb and lifted my hand up for me to examine closely. "See, Daddy, your hands are getting wrinkly and you are getting older. Are you going to die soon?" Delivered in utter innocence, wide-eyed, a serious question.

Well, my hands aren't that wrinkled, hardly at all in fact, but I said that I hoped that my end wasn't too near at hand. But it might happen, I told them. There could be an accident, or I could get very sick from a bad disease. Sometimes people just die, I explained, but chances were I'd live a good bit longer. And why did he want to know?

"I was just asking. You are getting old like grandma and grandpa, and someday you'll die, but first can you wait 'til I have little children so you can be their gran'pa, and we can all eat cookies and drink coffee milk together?"

How could I refuse a request like that?

I put them to bed in our evening ritual, which included dropping each of them onto their beds so they bounce a little, pulling the covers up to their necks, and being called back at least twice—for a fresh glass of water, for an extra hug or kiss, or maybe just to tease me and giggle. It is a fine way for them to go to sleep. Then I retired to my office in the basement to ponder the evening's subject.

Am I old? Am I going to die soon?

Well, I certainly hope not. But having children around makes me think that my own mortality is a little more certain now than I once thought. As I say, the bones and joints are all a little less resilient to the abuse I heap on them. I used to pride myself on having a strong back, being able to lift and haul heavy loads easily. But that was ten years ago. These days, every so often, I do something stupid like lift a really big rock up onto my garden wall, and my back reminds me that I am in my thirties. And while thirty-two may not be old, it is not as spry as eighteen or even twenty-five. So I should be grateful that I have only strained a muscle or pinched a nerve when my back twinges. A few generations ago I'd have been lucky to have survived long enough to have back problems. I expect that those ancestors of mine in fourteenth-century Europe who survived the plague did not complain about a sore lumbar, or knees that creaked on a cold morning.

I don't think of myself as old. On the other hand, I don't think of myself as young anymore. I feel comfortable where I am. Being in my thirties works for me. Young enough to do stupid things like hoist the wrong rock without destroying my back completely, old enough to know better. My parents used to tell me that I was born thirty-seven, that I was just waiting for my body to catch up with my mind. I still have five or so years left to that age, but I look forward to it with some anticipation. I wonder how the age will fit, if it will indeed be a perfect moment of body and mind in synchronicity.

When I was much younger, I was anxious to be a grown up. Each stage of life, each passing milestone was a victory, bringing me one step closer to the age I wanted to be, whatever that might have been. Getting out of second grade, from Miss Gray's class to Miss Pace's third-grade portable, was a grand step up. The day I walked out of my high school to catch the bus home, knowing it was for the last time, was an almost unbelievable moment of ecstasy.

And each day, as I grow a little wiser, as I move toward another goal, I feel good about it. It is a sense that each day brings a new experience, a new bit of knowledge, and a little bit more independence, even as my responsibilities to my wife, children, and the mortgage company grow. My only regret is highlighted by Max's question. Am I old? Am I going to die someday? The latter question has a resounding yes, I will die someday, and that is probably the ultimate disappointment, that I can not go on learning and experiencing forever. But if I can last long enough to sit at my kitchen table, drinking coffee milk and eating Oreo cookies with my grandchildren, that'd be fine by me.

Monsters

There is a modest-sized cove on the western shore of the island. Every day, the tourists come out in droves to lie in worship, or swim, or play. You must arrive early, if you want any hope of finding a shady spot for your car in the park's tiny lot, or of securing a clear plot of sand to spread out towels and toys and coolers, near the shade, near the toilets, and definitely near the ice cream stand.

The surf is a little tough to get through, kind of rolling over and under just as it hits the beach. While you aren't really at any great risk of drowning in the breakers, there's a better than even chance that they will pull your bathing suit down.

Once you get past that, the bottom slowly drops, changing from pinkish white sand to heads of coral and broken blocks of lava. Fish hover or dart in and out of the rocks, wondering if you've brought them food, or if you think that they are food. It must be a nervous existence for them.

Today there are twenty or thirty snorkelers in the water, a pair of scuba divers, and a crust of small children playing along the surf's edge. Max and his mother are building a sand fortress, with towers and parapets and great walls to withstand the mightiest enemy.

Fifty or sixty yards off-shore, out past the jam of bathers, Sarah is perched on an air mattress, one with the small window of clear plastic cut in, and she is peering intently into the blue-green to the reef below. Her father (me), decked out in fins, mask, and snorkel, and tied to her raft with a fifteen-foot cord, is hand-feeding fish, much to her delight. I can see her face, when I look up, and the smile of absolute delight is a treasure. This is one of my moments, one of my absolutely perfect and divine moments.

Finally, my poor lungs remind me that I must breathe, and I gently glide to the surface, exhaling through my snorkel, making a shower of warm water that sprays Sarah. She squeals, and laughs and begins to ask me if I saw all the same fish that she saw. The pink and blue ones, and the long ones that look like needles, and the funny round one with all the spikes on it. We make up names for the fish, like Bill and Ed and Henrietta. We name one really big one that keeps trying to hide under small rocks Buster because it is trying to bust up the rocks, according to Sarah. We examine the sea shells that I have been bringing up to her, and the little pile of coral sand, and I have a moment to catch my breath.

"Daddy," she asks, "can we go out farther?"

Looking back toward shore, I can see that we have drifted almost 100 yards out, and as I glance down in the water with my mask, I see that the bottom is starting to get a little hazy, a little dim, and I can tell that it is at least 15 feet down. Suddenly, a chill runs up my spine, sort of popping from the lumbar right up to the base of my skull one vertebra at a time, and I am intensely frightened. It feels exposed to be here, even this close to land. I cannot see much of my surroundings, and this is cause for some fear. I didn't realize in the pleasure of my child's company and the spirit of our adventure that we had come out so far.

The fear doesn't really have a name. It isn't Great White Sharks, although if I thought there was even a small chance I'd meet one, I would stay out of the water in anything smaller than an aircraft carrier. It isn't mythical sea monsters or a giant squid or even drowning. It is an unknown, indefinable trembling feeling that creeps up on me in a place where I know that there is so much beyond the range of my vision. Sometimes, being in that place doesn't bother me at all. But sometimes it terrifies me. And it can get much worse.

The first time I went scuba diving at night, I was holding myself back from the edge of panic. I did all of the relaxation breathing learned from our childbirth class as I bobbed at the surface, and then I dropped into the pitch darkness, with only a tiny flashlight and the phosphorescence to see by. I began to calm down, getting the feel of the experience, settling into a focused and relaxed state. And then the thing with the two-foot gaping mouth came blasting out of the darkness like a nightmare, and I was a fraction of a second from being on my way up and out of the water before I realized that it was the very manta ray I had come to see. Harmless, unless you happen to be plankton, and quite spectacular. Once you are sure that it isn't going to eat you.

"Daddy, can we go out farther?"

How do you tell your six-year-old child that you, the father, the protector, are feeling chicken? In the ocean, farther out from land than she can swim, and the Dad is scared. Dads aren't supposed to be scared, to be fearful. It is against the Dad's Code of Conduct.

I suppose everyone lives with some fears or terrors. I don't think I have any massive phobias. There are no situations that I can think of in which I simply freeze up and turn into a zombie—although I bet if a thirty-foot man-eating demon alien from Planet Cannibal landed in my yard, I'd react that way. But spiders, closed-in spaces, monsters, all the usual stuff doesn't really bother me.

It's just that every once in a while I realize that I am in a situation that I'm not really happy about. I park in a neighborhood where my chances of making it back to my car in one piece are slimmer than I'm used to. I drift much too far off-shore with a small child who cannot swim and is depending on me, and only when I am out a ways do I realize what sort of situation I am in. I feel a surge of panic, a spark of fear ready to burst into a full blaze given half a chance.

But I have uncovered one sure-fire method of coping, of maintaining my calm and cool for a few moments, just long enough to get out of the situation as best I can. It is simple, really. I just assume the *worst* possible result. Anything else that happens, then, will be a delightful surprise.

So as we drifted off the shore of that cove, I figured that I was going to die. A five-thousand-pound shark was going to come up and eat me, one limb at a time—sparing Sarah of course. No matter what I did, the odds of my getting back to shore were so small as to be not quite zero. So, completely confident in my impending demise, I looked at Sarah and said, "You bet honey, let's go out a little farther."

Coin of the Realm

On workdays, as I crawl down the freeway in the gridlock that characterizes commuting in Seattle, I listen to a news radio station. I rarely have time for the morning or evening paper, and I never seem to get around to watching the news on TV, so I make do with the half hour's commute to catch up on what's going on in the world.

I get weather, local, national, and international news, who is bombing whom this week, which former Soviet Republic has split off, and all the other tragedies of the day. There hardly ever seems to be anything good going on, but I am so jaded that I hardly notice that anymore.

The one part of the news that completely baffles me is the business and economic report. I guess it is aimed at the stock brokers and money lenders in our area, since it isn't presented in any terms that I can begin to fathom. I do understand what it means when Boeing lays off seven thousand people. When the school district issues bonds, my property taxes will rise. That makes sense. But then they go right to the Mystical Realm of Economic Indicators: the Dow, the Nikkei average, long bonds, short bonds, one-year and thirty-year T-bills and the value of the dollar versus the yen. The Beige book. The consumer confidence indicators. The whirlings and machinations of these things seems to hold major importance to "Business," how we gauge where the world is, and where we Americans sit in the overall picture.

To make matters more complex, my children often ask tough questions about the world economy. Like how much does that guinea pig cost, and do I have enough money in the piggy bank to buy it? The challenge is to give them a value system that they can both understand and use, something that is fairly meaningful to them. But what?

Simpler than it may seem. We use the World Big Mac Indicator.

If you want to explain economics to your child—like how much that bike costs—telling them that it is a hundred dollars is meaningless. A hundred anything is a big number to a child, no matter what the unit of measurement is, and a hundred and a million are both equally large. Instead, why not tell the children that the bike costs the same as thirty Big Macs, each with a side of fries and a medium soda. That is something a child can relate to.

For that matter, it can help adults understand the economy on a global scale. You want to know how well America is doing versus the foreign competition? Find a foreign tourist, and ask him how much that Big Mac, large fries, and a medium soda cost in his country. Then ask him if that is a lot of money. You'll see.

On vacation in Hawaii last year, I had dinner in a Japanese-style steak house, the kind where one chef comes out and juggles knives and pepper grinders for eight diners. Two of my dinner companions were Swedish tourists honeymooning in America. After the usual pleasantries, we got to talking about the U.S. and Sweden, and the subject of money came up. I asked if it was expensive to live in Sweden, and how it compared to the U.S. The husband's response, without more than a moment's hesitation, was to tell me that a Big Mac, fries, and a Coke cost about seven dollars at the current exchange rate, and that seemed to him like a lot for a hamburger. Last time I checked with my local Mickey D's back in Seattle, the same meal was about three bucks plus tax, without super-sizing. How much more basic can you get than that? This is proof positive that America is leading in the economic race, at least with Sweden.

I did a little research and found that in general terms, the Big Mac is cheaper in the U.S. than in any other country, including Japan, France, Italy, Germany, the former Soviet Union, Great Britain, Canada, and Australia.

Not fair, some of you will say. In some countries, the Big Mac is not available. Ah, well, these unfortunate countries obviously do not choose to live within the established economic norms and should be boycotted. If you need a reference point within these countries, there *are* other exchange mediums which can be compared. For example, to compare the U.S. with Kenya, you can use the price of a Kentucky Fried Chicken three-piece meal (the one with potatoes, coleslaw, and a biscuit).

My children are beginning to develop a sense for money, as they collect their allowances in exchange for making their beds, tidying up their rooms, feeding the cats, and other odds and ends in the chore department. It is a challenge to explain the meaning of money to them, especially when they feel a quarter is preferable to a dollar bill. To their way of thinking, since you can't stick a dollar into a gumball machine, quarters are a much better deal. They distinguish between coins and paper money as "cash" and "dollars." It gets even more confusing when we try to establish that a twenty-dollar bill is better than a one-dollar bill. My daughter says that if a twenty is worth more, it ought to be bigger and more impressive than a one.

I suppose that all children get some grasp of money eventually, just as they learn to read the hands of a clock and can begin to understand what I really mean when I say that I'll be there in a minute. But you have to start somewhere. If I can explain the value of money in terms of hamburgers and fries, I think they will understand. This will no doubt prepare them for the real world. Unless of course they grow into adulthood thinking that they can buy that new car with a truckload of Big Macs.

Sarah and the Beam

I sometimes find myself in those situations where I feel that I am giving up a portion of the limited time that is my life for no apparent good reason. Whether forced to sit in a lecture about slime molds or trapped at dinner with a uninteresting companion, I resent these intrusions, and I avoid them whenever I can.

I was once invited to be a board member of an educational foundation. One of my first acts was to attend a conference designed to pump us up into a frenzy of fund-raising. It was slow, dull torture, and before too long, I realized what a grave mistake I had made by agreeing to join.

The chairman of the board, a foolish man who thought that a red sports car would make his life better, ran through a few opening remarks, and then asked each of us to introduce ourselves. He also asked, in recognition of the board's goal of supporting the learning process, that we each describe the most important educational experience we had ever had.

At first, the stories were about some particularly wonderful teacher, an inspirational lecture. And then someone had to go and do it. The guy couldn't sit back, and speak in general terms of a magnificent lecture. He had to drop the name. He had to say Kissinger.

At that point, the rules changed. I could almost hear the noise of buzzing and popping in people's heads as they searched their memories for something really special. The discussion turned from best educational experience to a contest of one-upmanship. Who could come up with the most impressive story. People spoke of studying abroad, or with someone like Carl Sagan, of time spent at Harvard or Yale. It started to get tedious, and my life clock noted that I had already sacrificed two hours to this nonsense.

My turn arrived. I thought about telling a story about studying abroad, or even inventing a class that I had taken that no one else could possibly top—nude tap dancing with Marshall McLuhan. But instead, I told the story of my daughter and the beam.

At Sarah's school, in the middle of the playground sandbox, there's a large climber. It has two parts—one a low platform, easy for any child to clamber on. But the other half of the climber had been built high above the ground, with a crow's nest from which a child could survey the entire school. The crow's nest was the most popular place to play. It is only accessible by crossing a six-by-six beam, four feet above the sand. The school rule was that you had to be six years old or able to cross the beam to play in the crow's nest.

Sarah was five then and unable to maintain the balance needed to make the crossing. Four feet is a long way up when you are five. She tried and tried, but she kept falling off. It became quite an unhappy subject for her. Her friends were older, six or seven years old, and allowed to play in the crow's nest.

Most days, as we rode home from school together, Sarah would go on about the injustice of it all, as she brushed the sand from her knees all over my car. It wasn't fair, she would huff, that Kelly and Samantha and Gedney and Tesha could play in the crow's nest, just because they could cross the beam. It wasn't right and it wasn't fair and it hurt her feelings.

In my fatherly wisdom, I offered various takes on the unfortunate truth that life is indeed unfair. But that this was no excuse to stop trying. The answer to this, as you might expect, was most often a plumped-out lower lip and scowl, followed by a silent ride home.

But one day, one glorious day, as I pulled into the school parking lot, I saw Sarah, upright in the middle of the beam. She crept forward slowly, arms spread cruciform and waving up and down for balance. I actually held my breath, sitting in my car, watching and willing her across. She faltered a little but recovered and finally reached the crow's nest, a smile the size of Idaho spreading across her face.

I got out of the car, and ran to her, calling her name. She turned and saw me, and started screaming at the top of her lungs, *Daddy! I did it, I did it, I did it!!!!*

That was the best educational experience ever—watching my child learn that a difficult challenge can be overcome with patience and effort. Sarah has applied the same resolve to learning to cross the monkey bars, hang upside down from a tree branch, and even tap dance. I hope that the enthusiasm carries over into all of her learning, from math and science, to playing the piano and driving a car.

I felt a glow when I told that story. It was such a great joy to see Sarah grapple with a challenge, and triumph. To this day, when I feel stupid or incapable, I think of the image of her on that platform in her moment of absolute victory, and I find resolve to try again.

When I finished telling the story, I looked around the room at the other members. I saw a sea of glazed expressions. And then the next guy explained how he had studied with a Tibetan holy man. They had missed the point, I suppose, or perhaps the world is filled with too many people who gave up before they crossed the beam.

This Won't
Hurt a Bit

I hate needles. I can hardly stand having them stuck into me. At the dentist, I get my teeth drilled without benefit of anesthesia, rather than deal with the discomfort of having a needle stuck in my face (not to forget the added annoyance of drooling the rest of the day). I do not like getting shots, even in this day and age of teeny little disposable needles that you supposedly hardly feel. The idea of having any sort of steel pin jammed into my flesh does not sit well with me. And the discomfort of the lump of stuff that gets pumped in after it, making a painful spot on my arm that lasts for at least a week. That along with the "kindly" nurse mumbling silly things like "This won't hurt a bit." Sure, it won't hurt *her* at all.

The local blood bank likes to torture me with my dislike of needles, calling me every fifty-six days to remind me that it is time. I can hear the glee in their voices when they call, knowing that they have just ruined my day. I do go and donate, but I don't like it one bit. I have trained the staff at the blood center that it is normal for me to sweat and turn pale when I am donating, and if I look like I feel unwell and would rather be elsewhere, well it's because I feel unwell and would rather be elsewhere. But since I worked up enough courage to show up at the center and let them stick a needle directly into my vein, what the heck, may as well take a pint.

Now that I have children, and the school district has rules about vaccinations, I am not only required to go in and get my own shots every now and then but I have to take the children in for theirs. And I hate it.

One Thursday afternoon, I picked them up from school before the normal time. At first they were confused by my earlier-than-usual appearance. Then my daughter made the connection—today was the *day*, the day to visit the doctor's for the sole purpose of getting shots. She seemed pretty fine about it, not too frightened, even a little giggly. Which was good. I could do without the screaming, kicking horror of a small child terrified beyond even irrational thought.

Then she had to go and tell her little brother, announcing it as loud as an eight-year-old's lungs can manage: "MAXIE, TODAY IS THE DAY WE GET SHOT!" Max had been happily building a sand castle in the play yard outside his class room, when his ears were assailed by this news. You might as well have told him that his entire family had just been eaten by a pack of rabid squirrels. Max proceeded to have a complete core melt-down, and within minutes he was reduced to a mess, streams of snot and tears cascading down his face, while his sister sat and giggled nervously. In the car, Max moaned and cried a mantra, *Idonwannagetashot, Idonwannagetashot, Idonwan-nagetashot,* occasionally switching over to the alternate, *Itsgonnahurt, Itsgonnahurt, Itsgonnahurt. . . .*

The unfortunate truth about small children is that the extremes of their feelings and behavior are amplified by the presence of other small children. A single small child, crying and fussing, has no one to feed off of except herself. Add another small child, and everything gets magnified. It's a bit like putting the two parts of an A-bomb's uranium core together. One on its own sits and bubbles and churns. Add a second in even the general proximity, and things start heating up. But confine the two of them in the cab of a three-quarter-ton pickup, cheek to cheek with an adult, and the chain reaction starts.

Sarah was calm at first, and I had hoped that Max might be reassured by her stoic view. Instead, as his tears progressed from rivulet to tidal wave, Sarah decided that there was no reason not to join in. And the adult—me—was gripping the steering wheel hard enough to pop knuckles with each shriek and wail.

And this is the condition that all three of us were in when we arrived at the doctor's. I had to herd-carry-push the children through the door of the waiting room. Half a dozen people looked up to see what the ruckus was, and they stared hard at me as I struggled to control two bawling, panicking children. From the looks I got, you'd think that we were there to do an amputation. I felt about three inches tall, and I started apologizing to people.

"Getting a shot. No behavioral problems here, just scared of the needle." People with children automatically understood and their view of me became "Poor schmuck, better you than me."

I sat the children down, holding them both at once on my lap, and I told them that I understood exactly how they felt. In particular, I told them the story about getting a gamma globulin shot in my butt several years ago. It hurts bad enough, I explained, to get a shot in the rear end. But the nurse administering it had all the tenderness of a large truck, and I could not sit down comfortably for about two days.

This was enough to reduce them to giggles and snickers, thinking about their dad with a needle shoved into his hind end, and limping around in pain. It distracted them from their own impending date with the needle, and every few seconds, one of them would blurt out "You got a shot in the *butt!*" and we would all chuckle and laugh at my expense.

But the fun had to end. The nurse came, and the moment was upon us. Faced with the reality of two syringes, both were initially calm but very, very clear that they did not want to do this. They tried to negotiate their way out of it, as they do when they are sent to their room for shaving the cat or getting into the treat basket without permission. "I'll be good, please don't make me get a shot." I tried to explain that this was not a punishment for a crime, just good health care—a concept that holds no water with children who will eat dirt.

Sarah, perhaps realizing that there was no way out, volunteered to go first, and quite frankly, she took the experience with a show of bravado that was impressive, especially for her. Wipe, clean, shove, and it was over. She laughed and told her brother that it didn't really hurt at all. "Your turn, Max. Be brave," she counseled. "It'll be over in a second."

Regardless of what Sarah said, the needles must have looked like three-eighths-inch tungsten-carbide drill bits to Max, because my son was possessed at that very moment by a demon from the lowest bowels of hell, and was reduced to a state somewhere between sheer terror and being really pissed-off. He struggled and kicked, and declared, "I'm not gettin' a shot. No, no, NO-NO-NO!" I had to pin him down, and even then it was like wrestling with an angry python. I finally got a lock on him and held him as tight as I could as the nurse ran through the routine. All the time, Max continued to scream and kick, and made several tries at biting me. My tie was twisted around the two of us, my shins were barked and bruised from where he was scrambling, and I am sure my pulse crested over a hundred and fifty. Max wasn't looking much better. But at least he didn't pee on me.

And then it was over. He sniffled a few times as the last tear slid down his cheek and slowly his calm returned. The nurse offered a choice of Snoopy or Garfield Band-Aids, and a Tootsie Pop.

By the time we got home that evening, the terror of the needle had been forgotten and they had both forgiven me (with the help of two very large bowls of vanilla ice cream). Max was feeling pretty pleased with himself, having braved the experience and survived. He strutted around the house, sporting a sticker from the doctor that said I GOT A SHOT TODAY! and telling his mother how brave he had been, bragging on himself and his nerve in the face of the terrible needle. In a loud voice, over dinner, he proclaimed that "I'm getting really good at shots! They don't scare me anymore!"

His mother praised him, kissing him lightly on the cheek. She looked at me and smiled. "So it went pretty well? He was good?"

I rolled up the legs of my trousers and displayed the fresh purple welts on my shins. "Yeah," I said, "he was good. And if that was good, may I be delivered from bad."

And Never
the Twain
Shall Meet

When you grow up, you move out of the house—your parents' house, where you have lived according to their rules, standards, and ideas. What they want for dinner, what color they want to paint the living room, whether or not Aunt Harriet comes to stay for three weeks in the summer, sleeping in your room, leaving you with the lumpy sofa bed in the family room. As a child, your parent's home was a citadel, protecting you from the unknowns beyond its walls. But with the passage of time, sometimes it feels as much a prison as a sanctuary.

At last you step out into the real world, with college or high school behind you, getting a job, settling into your own apartment or house. Perhaps you have roommates to share the expense of housing, but suddenly the rules are totally within your control. It is pure, undiluted freedom, a heady brew, all yours in a place of your own. You want to leave underwear on the floor, dishes in the sink, shaving stubble on the bathroom counter, go right ahead. Violate all the rules of hygiene and cleanliness that you lived by for so long. Enjoy this time while you can. It passes too quickly. This is what you have been waiting for, a chance to be an adult and practice self-determination unfettered by a curfew or any other creature's demands.

Which means that getting married may come as a nasty surprise. In the instant that passes as you move through the words "I do," your life gets bonded to another. The structure of your thought and language shifts suddenly like a brief jolt on a fault line, and "yours" becomes "ours," as in "our joint checking account" or "our bathroom." With the bathroom, though, *she* may say that it is "ours" but she darn well means "hers."

For me, this was the greatest adjustment required by marriage. I had been so intently focused on getting out of my parents' house that the idea of voluntarily agreeing to give up any measure of my newly acquired self-determination was appalling. To agree to cohabitate and cooperate with another human, being intimate on a daily basis, being required to surrender the sole occupancy of my bathroom, to let her spend my money on foolish things like a mortgage, to have to time-share the TV remote, not to mention closet space—these and many other things necessitated a serious change in my attitude.

Of course, it wasn't and isn't all that bad. I did ask my wife to marry me of my own free will, and I showed up at the church as I was directed to, so I can't rightly blame it all on her. But there are days when I wonder how we manage it. It is such a juggling act.

My friend Tom, and his wife, Lucy, are two of the most content and happy people I know. Especially in their marriage. They have four sons, all of whom are great kids, and they seem to get along so completely and perfectly. It is possible that they are the match created in the machine shop of heaven.

I've wondered how two people can make a relationship work so well. I've seen a lot of marriages end in divorce, and more than a few that do not seem to have much love in them. So when a good marriage comes along, I try and divine the secret formula for its success. Early in my own marriage, when I was still grumpy about the TV remote control issue, I asked Tom to impart the wisdom behind the success of his relationship to me.

Tom had a simple explanation. The two of them, Tom and Lucy, agreed early on to separate responsibility for life's decisions, each taking a segment and not interfering with the other's bailiwick, unless asked to "consult" in an nonbinding, advisory role. Tom says that Lucy chose to make all of what she described as the "simple decisions," and left it to Tom to wrestle with the meatier issues of their life together. I was impressed when I heard this. Lucy had never struck me as the kind of woman to sit back and play a passive role in anything. I said as much, and Tom smiled. Then he explained what this arrangement really meant.

Simple decisions were things such as: where they lived, where they worked, how they spent their money, how their four sons were to be raised, what color to paint the house, which car they drove. Important decisions were the much more weighty and significant problems of a couple's life together: nuclear disarmament, the defeat of World Communism, famine relief, the Savings & Loan bailout, world peace, and the hole in the ozone layer.

I ran into Tom about a year ago and asked him how he was doing with his half of the decisions. He said that up until recently, his wife was having a much greater degree of success with her area than he was, but the fall of the Berlin Wall and the dismantling of American and Soviet nuclear warheads in recent years have made him feel much better about his own responsibilities.

I have always tried to remember that story when things tend to seem a little more complicated. My wife and I have never formally defined our roles; we just sort of fell into a status quo of duties. Somehow it is understood that *these* things are for me to do, and *those* things are hers.

If it's heavy and apt to cause a hernia, I lift it. If it is crawling across the floor in a threatening manner, if it needs to be dead, I kill it. Once it's dead, I body-bag and bury it. If it's disgusting, dirty, smelly, and needs to be taken out to the trash, I deal with it. If it involves electricity, plumbing, or the structural integrity of our home, as in "If we knock that wall out, will the house collapse?" I get to make the call. You can't get much more simple that that.

Marie's duties are equally straightforward. If it requires patience and concentration, such as dealing with the household accounts, she tallies and balances it. If it requires discerning taste, Marie deals with it. If it relates to the color we paint the house, Marie decides. In fact, if it involves more than one primary color, such as which tie I am allowed to wear with which shirt, it falls outside my responsibilities, and into hers (getting dressed on mornings when she is gone are a frightening experience—I keep a list that she has thoughtfully provided of dressing do's and don'ts pinned up in my closet). If it involves our social calendar, she schedules it. If it needs to be tucked in with hospital corners, she tucks it.

It is a very Yin and Yang sort of arrangement. In these over-simplified generalizations, I can find clear solutions to many of my daily dilemmas. I ponder the question of the day, and ask if it relates to lifting a heavy object or murdering a spider? And if the answer is no, I am able to arrive at a solution. It is, simply put, *her* problem.

Mother
Out-Law

G etting married is a fusion reaction.
Two lives, moving along separate paths, collide at exactly the right point in space and time, in just the right way. Instead of bouncing off each other like human-sized billiard balls, the force and nature of the meeting is just right to cause fusion. Two separate lives become one, a shared experience, bound by the laws of man if not of physics.

As any physics student will tell you, a fusion reaction produces side effects. In a classic fusion reaction—a hydrogen bomb, for example—the side effects result in the vaporizing and leveling of huge tracts of real estate and people and the polluting of the landscape with radioactive fallout. In the case of marriage, the effect is the linking of two personalities and all their baggage—a combination which can be infinitely more dangerous.

Once you have become a married person, you will notice that the requirement of sharing and integrating only begins when you sign the license. And it certainly doesn't end with you and your spouse and how you agree on running the household.

Of course, I am speaking of in-laws. Or, as my mother likes to say, out-laws.

Among all the other things you must address in your marriage—how you squeeze the toothpaste tube, if you leave your dishes in the sink or stow them in the dishwasher, whether you turn your socks right side out before you dump them in the laundry hamper—in addition to all that, you will also have the added issue of getting to know your in-laws and fitting yourself into their family. Assuming that they will let you. Assuming that you *want* to.

This is not always an easy task. It is possible that your in-laws are deserving of a four-and-a-half chain saw rating on the psycho scale, where one is a Ward Cleaver and a five is Norman Bates. Or perhaps they are just not your sort of people—they eat with their feet, for example. Or maybe you just don't like them, and they don't like you, either. What will you do?

One option is not to have gotten into the fix in the first place. The simplest approach here is to take her parents on the first date, so as to scope them and her out at the same time. You won't get to dessert before you find out if either they or their daughter are not your cup of tea. Of course, this puts a headlock on the chances of doing any spooning after dinner, so you'll have to treat the date strictly as a reconnaissance mission and save the lip lock for another time.

You might be too far along for that. Maybe you got through all the courting part, bought the rings, made the proposal and all that, and only then did you realize what sort of family you are marrying into. Well, barring the fact that you are a tetch slow in the head, if you've gone that far, you can't do much. Calling it off takes a great deal of courage. The easiest way out here is not to show up for the wedding. It is rather rude, so you should at least send a note of explanation—"Honey, I love you, but your parents are like those bits of popcorn that get stuck under your gum line. Sorry." Not very subtle or kind, but it does the job.

A more reasonable reaction to the potential in-laws from hell is to shrug and not worry about them. You can remind yourself that you married her, not her family. Who cares if her mother looks like Jimmy Hoffa and acts like Godzilla on a bad scale day? So what if her dad looks like her mother and his business is built on the discreet and reasonably priced disposal of PCBs in the local reservoir. Nobody's perfect, right? Sure, a less-than-friendly relationship with your in-laws can make your marriage difficult, not to forget the possibility of those family events like Christmas and Thanksgiving turning into nightmares.

But you're a tough guy.

You can take it.

For the next twenty-five years.

Better you than me.

If you love her, and you aren't a complete fool, you had best go ahead and do the smart thing and get married. You can most probably survive whatever insanity her parents may throw at you. And if not, you can always move to the opposite end of the country, someplace where no major airline flies, now or anytime in the distant future, say Sequim, Washington, or Edna, Texas.

Odds are that your in-laws will be decent enough people, and getting to know them will be the biggest problem you've got to cope with. Maybe "problem" isn't the right word. Better to say "challenge," since any relationship requires work and attention. On the positive side, you can take comfort in knowing that your in-laws will also be trying to integrate themselves into your family. And you're probably going to have more success when both parties are making an effort.

In the case of my extended family, the worst problem I have is holiday meals. I feel obliged to show up at both my mother's and my in-laws' for two separate Thanksgivings, with just enough time in between to digest a little. I invariably end that particular day feeling like I have eaten two entire turkeys, and a bloated sideboard of mashed potatoes and pumpkin pie and whipped cream. Christmas is the same. In our extended family, we now have four distinct Yuletide celebrations. Since my folks are divorced, we celebrate once with my mother, once with my father, have a family event with just my wife, kids, and me, and then a trip to my in-laws' for still more ripping and tearing of wrapping paper.

From the first meeting, when I showed up at their house for dinner, with my stomach tied into a sheep shank knot, through the wedding, the birth of grandchildren, and all the life that has come since the first dinner together, we have built a good family with my in-laws. I have become comfortable with them, and I love them both very much. But then again, they are hard people not to love. All things considered, I feel pretty lucky—my in-laws are nice people, easy to be with and around, and much loved by their grandchildren.

And besides, they don't charge for baby-sitting.

Snoring

I don't sleep much, but when I do, I sleep with a vengeance. I have slept through hundred-mile-per-hour windstorms and 6.0 magnitude earthquakes. During that earthquake (in Tokyo), my parents rushed out of the hotel, only realizing after the quake was over that I was still inside, fast asleep. When I get to slumber land, it's as though my brain has been disconnected from my senses, covered in Saran Wrap, and put in cold storage for the night.

Most mornings, I am awakened from this coma by my wife with a kiss on the cheek and a command to arise. "Get up," she says cheerfully. "It's time to go to work, to be a useful cog on the wheel of production that is our socio-economic strength." Well, she doesn't really say it quite that way, but that is what she means. I often note, as I rub the sleep from my eyes, that my ribs are sore.

That means I have been snoring, and that Marie has spent

part of the night sticking an elbow into my side to get me to roll over into a different position, on my side or stomach, in hopes that I won't snore. Snoring is a real pain for both of us. As luck would have it, my wife is a very light sleeper. She must have complete darkness, silence, and stillness. When the alarm goes off in the morning, she is awakened by the tiny click it makes just before the music comes on. Marie is easily wakened by almost any noise, like the cats cleaning themselves in the living room. I believe tectonic-plate movement in Bolivia and the gravitational pull of Pluto would probably wake her too, but I can't prove it.

But whatever else may keep her awake at night, my snoring tops it all. Get me lying on my back, and my uvula begins to vibrate. The frequency at which I snore seems to resonate with some natural oscillation within Marie's body and soul, causing pain and discomfort.

I did not believe that I was a snorer up until recently. For the first few years of our marriage, my wife would whack me and tell me that I was snoring. Waking slightly, I would listen and hear nothing, so I denied everything and went back to sleep— and snoring. Then one night, a couple of years ago, I actually woke myself up with the noise.

That was a shock. Me? Snore? I don't snore. Do I? Yeah, you bet I do.

I take some consolation in the fact that I am a rank amateur, compared with some people I know. My father-in-law, for example, used to snore at a world-class Olympic Gold Medal level. I have slept on the hide-a-bed at his house, and I could hear him from down the hall. The house seemed to shake every time he struggled for breath.

My friend Terry snores like a radial arm saw cutting through galvanized sheet tin. I have actually considered sleeping in his yard when visiting, rather than lying awake in the guest room wondering if the ceiling was going to cave in.

Terry has lifted snoring to a fine art. He snores like what the army calls harassment fire—that's when you fire your artillery at odd intervals all night, to keep the enemy awake and guessing when the next round is going to fall. Terry does that. He'll snore for a bit, then quiet down, lulling you into a false sense of security. Just as you are getting back to sleep, BOOM, the hank-snurf-HANH! hits, and you're awake again, wondering if you'll ever get to sleep, and contemplating the cost of holding a pillow over his face—just for a couple of minutes.

Now that I recognize that I snore, I sympathize with my wife. I am told that there is help for those of us who are afflicted. You can have your sinuses reamed, smashed, sliced, and reconfigured to allow a more even airflow. Imagine lying on your back, awake but dull from Valium, as a doctor hovers over your face with a chisel and a three-pound mallet. Imagine having a large chunk of your septum pulled out, reshaped, and sewn back in, all to a little Mozart and Vivaldi. Imagine spending three days with what feels like a golf ball shoved up your nose.

Or for a slightly larger fee, a surgeon will chop, channel, and Bondo your uvula and soft palette. Very high tech, all laser surgery. Hurts like a mother-jumper. And he'll do it as often as it takes to get it right. He'll even throw in a block of plastic, custom molded to your mouth, that will hold your jaw in just the right way to keep you from snoring.

I highly recommend that Terry look into this procedure. As for myself, I'd rather sleep on the couch.

Potty
Training

When my youngest child, Max, was four, he reached that stage in his life where he was finally aware of most of the functions of his body. The latest discovery has been that wet pants are uncomfortable things.

We have already potty-trained one child, so of course we are experts in the field of coprothology (the unofficial study of impending bowel movement recognition). I now recognize the "I gotta pee but I don't want to stop what I'm doing" dance, where the child twists and turns, grasping his groin, trying to postpone the inevitable.

For a long time, we teetered on the edge of house-breaking Max. It was frustrating at times. But I knew in my heart of hearts that every child does eventually figure out how to use the toilet. As my mother-in-law says, "You don't see too many adults in diapers, now do you?" Well, I am not entirely sure if that is a true statement or not, but I have to admit that personally I don't know any adults who wear diapers or training pants.

Finally the toilet-training exodus has begun. From the realm of diapers and the lingering ammonia smell that emanates from the diaper pail, we have traveled through the world of pull-ups, past training pants, and into the ultimate goal of small boys everywhere, the "Big Boy Batman Panties." Max was very excited by the thought of wearing the midget Y-fronts stashed in his diaper drawer. He knew that they were there, and he coveted them in an almost sinful fashion. His progress toward them was in fits and starts, marred by moments of backsliding, and crowned by great triumphs.

One night, about a year ago, after he had been dressed in his pj's, he explained that he, of his own free will, with no adult coercion, wished to visit the facilities.

And he did!

And he did again the next morning!

My wife and I high-fived each other, singing the praises of freedom from the life of toting diapers and wipes everywhere we went.

Max's reward that morning was to be allowed to wear a pair of pull-ups to school. Pull-ups, for those of you not in the parental know, are disposable training pants. They are considerably less bulky than cloth or disposable diapers, and Max suddenly looked a lot less like one of those round-bottomed toys that bounce back when you push them over. Max was very proud, and when we got to school, he went to see Miss Jami, his favorite teacher, and he announced, pulling his blue jeans down to display the pull-ups, that *he* had used the potty that morning *and* last night.

We were halfway there.

And then, Max elected to use the potty for that other bodily function. In a word, he pooped. On the toilet. Praise to the Powers that made us, and pass the underwear.

Truth is, though, his initial fascination with using the toilet faded rather quickly after that. I suspect that he soon realized that parental praise and Batman panties were the total extent of the reward. Big-boy panties are enticing, but what I think he really wanted was to be allowed to drive my pickup truck. In the meantime, my wife and I racked our brains for ongoing methods of persuasion that would prod him in the right direction without putting undue pressure on him. I have heard from experts and other parents that you don't want to pressure a child into potty-training, as it may cause problems later.

Like what?

If I had pushed him to use the toilet, would I turn on the news one evening fifteen years from now and discover that some college freshman with the same last name as mine is on top of a dorm building with a diaper on, shooting coeds in the butt with a Daisy BB rifle? Or perhaps an unpleasant potty-training experience is what gives birth to a desire to attend law school or enter politics.

Marie and I finally settled on the direct approach. We told Max that there would be no more diapers, only cloth training pants, which slow down but do not hold a healthy pee or poop. When wet or dirty, they are very uncomfortable. And I had a man-to-man chat about it with him. I said, "Max, I want you to use the toilet. It would make me very happy, and I will be very proud of you. I can't let you drive the truck or use power tools until you're house-broken." He nodded that he understood, and promised to try. End of discussion.

Shortly thereafter, Max got down from the dinner table, and walked into the bathroom with a look of purpose in his eyes. Marie and I stood at the end of the hall watching very quietly, so he wouldn't know that we were there. He fumbled with his trousers and training pants, finally getting them down to his knees. With some difficulty, he managed to get all of his clothes arranged, take aim, and urinate. My wife and I cheered and clapped, and when Max heard us, he turned with a smile and said, "I used the potty."

I've never asked my parents how they broke me of the diaper pail. I do know that the day I first agreed to use the potty was also a heralded event. In response to Max's success, my father sent me a scrap of paper. It read: "Joy! Hunter used the potty today!"

I realize that a fixation with a child's toilet habits may seem a bit strange. But it is all part of being a parent. The job description for me as a parent is to prepare my children to leave me and make their way into the world on their own. My own parents have warned me several times to enjoy this time of the children's lives, because it will be over all too soon. In the meantime, we work on the potty-training, covering our mouths when we cough, washing our hands before dinner, brushing our teeth, and saying please and thank you. Minimal human functions and social behaviors.

I realize that my wife and I are passing along a tradition of sorts to our children. We are teaching them to be adults in much the same manner as our parents taught us. Never mind family heritage, genealogy, or history. We're talking the fundamentals here. We are passing on the most basic set of instructions, unchanging in its essential form from one generation to the next. In effect, Max's triumph is the current culmination of uncounted generations of Fulghums and Wolfangers striving toward the goal of big-boy or -girl panties.

I think of it as a type of heritage. I can say, "Son, you have your mother's eyes, your father's hair, and you pee like your great-uncle Norman."

Mailboxes

The new mailbox has arrived.

And it's not just any old mailbox. It is an official United States Postal Service NDCBU mailbox. Based on the way the thing looks, NDCBU must stand for NUCLEAR DETONATION-CHEMICAL-BIOLOGICAL UNIT. Made of steel, mounted with big, healthy-looking bolts to a concrete pad. Battleship gray. It looks mean. It must have been designed for use in Desert Storm, to ensure that even a direct Scud hit wouldn't keep old Stormin' Norman from getting offers to publish his memoirs. It's even more efficient, an eight-seater, so the safety of our treasured correspondence is now ensured for not only me but also for seven of my neighbors. For the moment, the USPS, that most evilly maligned of agencies, has redeemed itself, in my eyes at least.

You see, this mailbox is the seventh one we have had at this house. Let's hope it lasts a bit longer than its antecedents. When we first moved in, we never noticed that all of the mailboxes on the street were in pretty sad shape, particularly those closest to the oncoming traffic. I just wrote it off to poor driving on the part of the mail carrier.

Our own mailbox was on its last legs, so I went out and bought a really nice one for twenty bucks at the hardware store. Mounted it on a brand-new wooden post. It looked really nice. I even put our name and address on it in fancy stick-on letters. Just so the pizza guy could find us.

Two weeks later, I woke up about two in the morning, feeling more than hearing a *thwonk-wanga* kind of noise. I listened for a minute, heard a car go by, and went back to sleep. The next morning, as I backed down the driveway, I saw the source of the noise. My mailbox. Bearing an imprint shaped strangely like a baseball bat.

Not to worry, I thought. I drove to the hardware store and bought another twenty dollar mailbox. Put the numbers and name back on, with the same shiny stick-on letters.

Cut to ten days later. I back out of the driveway. The mailbox is again destroyed. Suddenly it dawns on me why all the mailboxes on the street are beat up. Well, I am too smart for any punk kid. I got a crush-resistant, high-impact plastic mailbox. The kind of mailbox the astronauts would have taken to the moon. Guaranteed to resist baseball bats.

It did. The baseball bat didn't even scratch it. But when they backed their car over the box and post, snapping it off at the base, they also made sure they drove over the box itself. Even high-impact plastic isn't capable of surviving two tons of automobile.

So, now I had lost my box *and* post. Not to be bested by vandals, I got a two-inch-square steel bar, six feet long, which I drove three feet into the ground. Right through a telephone line. Helpful tip. When you live in a neighborhood with underground utilities, call before you dig. I mounted another plastic mailbox on the post. I didn't even bother putting our name and number on it. I wanted to give it a road test before I went to the trouble.

Three weeks later, the box was still there. It had clearly taken a hit or two, but it was far too tough for a mere baseball bat. Unfortunately, it was not hacksaw resistant. This time, the little buggers actually sawed the whole front end off the box. On a rainy day, no less. The mail carrier, in all of his wisdom, left the mail there to get soaked, along with a nice little note that said that vandalism was truly a shame, but "Mr. Fulghum, get a new mailbox."

I understand the mentality of the vandalism-intent teenage male. The urge to go out in the wee hours with your buddies (in someone else's car), and run around acting crazy and stupid is part of the basic wiring of the male of our species. My mother, bless her long-suffering patience, got more than one late-night phone call from officer Friendly of the Seattle Police Department, inquiring if she might know the whereabouts of her number-two son. The officer knew, of course, that I was locked in the back of his squad car, feeling very stupid and not a little frightened.

My partners in crime, Steve, Lewis, Chris (the latter of whom is rumored to work for the National Security Agency, performing who knows what sort of mischief), and I spent more than a few evenings dismembering mailboxes ourselves, although we were more inclined to use explosives than baseball bats. The effect of detonating a large charge of homemade black powder in a confined space was oh-so-satisfying, not to mention the joy of knowing that we had awakened every neighbor in a four-block radius.

Of course, destroying mailboxes was probably the least of our offenses against society, but in the interest of not encouraging today's teenagers, I shall refrain from providing a detailed list. Suffice it to say that it is a minor miracle that somehow I avoided being shot or arrested by the local constabulary, and I arrived at adulthood relatively unscathed.

My history made me quite aware of the mindset of my mailbox adversary. I have met him, and he is I, fifteen years ago. But just because I understand his drives and nature does not mean that I will sit back and let it go, especially when I am trying to read a damp copy of National Geographic. The annoyance was just too much. It is depressing enough when I drive down my street in a constant downpour, reminding myself that I have chosen to live in the Pacific Northwest. Pulling up to my driveway and seeing the vandalized remains of my mailbox, knowing that the mail is soaked once again, really pissed me off.

I progressed to schemes involving booby traps, exploding mailboxes, and all-night vigils, hiding in the brush in wait. Visions of armor-plated mailboxes, set in six inches of reinforced concrete, danced in my dreams as I drifted off to sleep each night. I even considered filling the box with concrete, just to have the satisfaction of knowing that it might break the bat. Maybe even the batter's wrists, too. Or perhaps he would vibrate from stem to stern like some Looney Tunes cartoon character.

In the meantime, my neighbor, Charlie Brown (honest!), had

taken the direct and intelligent approach. He called the local post office, complained long and loud, filed a police report, and then demanded that the postmaster do something. He got seven neighbors, including me, to sign a petition asking that something be done. And strangely enough, the postal service came out and installed our explosion-proof mailbox. They even installed a larger box next to it for parcels. At no charge. End of story. It's almost disappointingly anticlimactic.

To celebrate, I think I'll go run over my old mailbox. After all, I wouldn't want it to think it had just been made obsolete. Better it should die a soldier's death, in the line of fire, standing firm to the last.

The God of
Barbeque

My father-in-law leads a secret life. In the everyday world of mere mortals he works as a mild-mannered real estate agent. He takes good care of his yard, doesn't play loud music, doesn't have wild parties. But this is just a clever cover for his true identity. Where Thor, God of Thunder, carries the great hammer, John Edward Wolfanger stands over a cast-iron barbeque, with the sacred fork in one hand and the holy spatula in the other, as the God of Barbeque.

When you pray for the coal to light the first time, you are praying to John. When you wish for a fair wind (that the wind would shift and blow the smoke out of your face), your wish is carried by the breeze to the ears of John. Just make sure you speak on his good side. And when you guess that the steak is medium rare, it is within the power of John the Barbeque God to make a liar of you, if he is displeased with you.

I believe that everyone in this world must have at least one thing for which they have a true gift. Some people are virtuoso violinists, others are brilliant scientists, still others have the gift of art. John has been given the gift of barbeque.

John can breathe life into the most sullen pile of charcoal, teasing it into a satisfying glow of hot carbon, and when the fire is just so, he can take any piece of meat you might care to name—beefsteak, fish, entire Thanksgiving turkeys, or wombat fillet—and cook them perfectly, so that they are tender, juicy, and seasoned to perfection. It is an amazing talent, one which he has passed on to his daughter but not to me, alas. I haven't the right stuff.

Just because I can't run the barbeque doesn't mean I don't try. I've spent many an early summer evening bathed in sooty fumes, so that I smell like I've been rolled in a coal bunker, fighting to nurture a fire with minimal life signs. In spite of myself, my old barbeque and I have churned out eleven years' worth of hamburgers, steaks, hot dogs, chicken, and ribs—a not insubstantial mound of animal parts.

Recently my poor old barbeque bit the dust. All those years under the Fulghum Quality Maintenance Plan (that is, sort of occasionally cleaning it, and leaving it more or less out of the rain) have proven too much for it, and the bottom finally rusted through. Time, I thought, to acquire a new barbeque to abuse and mistreat. My wife (without telling me) decided to order a good barbeque grill, just like her dad's. I think her theory was for what it cost, I'd be more likely to take good care of it.

Arriving home one day, I discovered a one-hundred-pound box of metal parts and screws awaiting my attention. The new barbeque—some assembly required—complete with rotisserie.

Somehow, I managed to get it put together with only a small handful of the parts left over, and my wife decided that we'd break it in on Father's Day, by smoking an entire turkey for the consumption of the whole family—including my father-in-law, the Barbeque God.

Such situations are designed to provoke seizures. In all my life, I had never used a rotisserie, much less smoked a twelve-pound turkey. The first test drive on the new grill, and instead of a nice, safe run through a couple of steaks, we were going four-wheeling in front of the most demanding of audiences.

To my surprise, I got the fire burning and the turkey skewered, and I even figured out how to get it onto the grill without any more damage than a couple of minor burns on my knuckles. I was even prouder of myself when I discovered how to get the bird balanced on the spit so that the drive motor could actually rotate it at a fairly even speed. It only took three tries, and aside from the fact that the bird looked as though it had been in a twelve-round bout with Mike Tyson, I felt pretty good about it. I wandered off to let the grill do its work.

Checking back thirty minutes later, I discovered an important point about the barbeque—that the spit, which is a three-piece unit, will come apart if not properly tightened up. Upon opening the lid to inspect the turkey's progress, I discovered the bird dangerously dangling less than an inch above the bed of coals—most of which had been extinguished by the drippings and the avalanche of celery and onion stuffing which had exploded from the turkey. The spit, slowly coming undone, rotated every few seconds with a labored and sickening *hhuunnnn-thunk,* like a busted axle. The side that was closest to the heat had begun to cook quite nicely, where the other was still raw and plucked looking.

Thank heaven for vice-grips and leather gloves. I rescued the turkey from the sputtering and grinding inferno, and tightened up every last part of the spit, tied the bird up to keep the wings and legs from dragging, and set about trying to salvage the fire. My wife watched me with an odd mix of amusement and nervousness, and I volunteered that it was not too late to take her parents out to dinner. I'd have just enough time to bury the turkey in an unmarked grave in the backyard and hide the barbeque in the garage before they arrived.

But Marie does not so easily abandon projects. At my suggestion of throwing the towel (and the turkey) in, she gave me her "don't even think about it" look, a look that is calculated to make me wish I'd kept my mouth shut. With this in mind I set myself to the task at hand, and got everything running in more or less smooth order, just moments before the in-laws arrived.

I felt a little like I had broken my mother's favorite piece of china and glued it back together, hoping she wouldn't notice. I could feel the presence of the Barbeque God as John strode across my deck, his finely polished boots sending daggers of light into my eyes. I briefly considered throwing myself at his feet and begging his advice and help in salvaging the supper. But I held back, cockily trusting my luck to hold long enough for the bird to cook.

The first time I stepped away from the grill, I watched John through the kitchen window carefully inspecting the barbeque, examining the quality of my assembly job, sizing up how well I had tightened nuts and bolts, before he gently opened the lid.

I held my breath, sure that he would discover the mutilated and burnt corpse of the bird, sitting directly on the bed of now-dead coals, being slapped every few seconds by the mangled end of the rotisserie.

Sometimes miracles happen. Maybe it was the aura of the Barbeque God, maybe it was my luck coming through. Either way, the turkey was gently rotating over the fire, sizzling and sputtering, and making an aroma that was almost fit for the deity present. John looked the situation over, adjusted two or three charcoal briquettes to better spots, and lowered the lid with a satisfied nod of his head.

And the turkey was delicious.

Like Father, Like Son

Putting John in the ground, perhaps fifty yards from where my own father will end his days, has a flavor to it that I find appropriate. Someday, right here, I will stand over another open hole, and watch my father being lowered into the earth, and I will finally be without a dad. I do not look forward to the day, I hope it does not come soon, but I think that I am prepared for this ultimate and necessary task by the fact that I have already buried one father.

The blessing of a father, to provide a male influence in a son's life, is not at all a given in every child's life. My parents decided some twenty-four years ago that theirs was not a match made in heaven, and that after ten or twelve years of marriage, it was time to part company. A couple of years later, my mother was married to John, a man as different from my father as night is from day, and yet similar in so many ways.

John's eldest daughter and I stood at the bar during my brother's wedding about four years back. She and I have been good friends for a long time, in spite of the ten years' difference in our ages. She was in a contemplative mood, and after a bit, she revealed what was troubling her. "You got the best years of my dad," she said, her eyes cast down to her drink.

I had no response. I could not deny it, because it was true, and I would not insult her intelligence with a phony denial. On the other hand, admitting that this was true would have been insensitive. So I responded as I could, which was to mumble a few platitudes and change the subject.

John was a nuclear physicist who worked on defense and nuclear projects for many years before confronting the ethical dilemma that his work posed. Eventually, he left Boeing and went to work for the Seattle Community College District as a teacher. He was remarkable at teaching, a natural at invigorating students with the wonders of science that he saw in the world around him. My mother has said on more than one occasion that John could make an education out of any event, no matter how simple.

John taught me about materials and crystals and atomic structures while he and I were breaking up an old concrete walkway with sixteen-pound sledgehammers. An afternoon spent rewiring a backdoor light turned into a discussion of lasers and ions and electron flow. We spoke long and often about the universe, from the Big Bang to just what infinity might really mean. The first time I looked through a telescope was with John. He took me to the University of Washington, and we saw the Galilean moons of Jupiter.

John's explanations of the world bore fruit in my life. I grew up to become an engineer, and spend my days working with lasers and fiber optics and communications. As I go through even the mundane aspects of my job routine, there is still a certain wonder in it all, that all of these bits and pieces of the world fit together in a magnificent system of science and mathematics and ideas.

By contrast, my father is a philosopher, a thinker in his own right, and as fascinated by life and people as John was intrigued by science. My dad looks for wonders in the people around him, in small events of life that can have big meaning—the meaning *in* life, as he likes to say, not the meaning *of* life.

For all of my childhood, he was a larger-than-life character, often with an easy smile on his face, or a faraway look that said he was pondering something. I was in awe of him for many years. I even thought when I was just a little boy that my father was really Saul Steinberg.

We used to have a coffee table book (but no coffee table upon which to place it), a book that was huge to a five-year-old, with a wonderfully bright yellow cloth cover. The inside was filled with fanciful line drawings of people and places and things, subways, men in bars, all very stylized and very appealing to me. They were more like cartoons than anything else. I spent hours looking at it, imagining what the drawings meant, and eventually I had read it so much that my parents just gave it to me. It became part of my collection of story books.

I was certain for many years that my father had drawn the pictures in the book. He was, after all, an art teacher, he drew pictures, and the book was full of pictures drawn by an artist. QED, my father had drawn the book. Quite reasonable logic for a small boy.

In reality, the book was a collection of drawings by Stein-berg, called *Life* if I remember correctly. I never actually men-tioned that Saul Steinberg was my father to anyone, and I don't ever recall being told any differently. I think that one day, after I had learned to read, I finally understood. Sort of a "Well, how about that," kind of revelation.

It is difficult to quantify a man like my father. He is a com-plicated mix of ideas, talents, professions, and emotions. Writer, speaker, teacher, artist, and minister are but a few of the titles I can assign to him. At his very core, though, is a man with a unique world view, as well as an ability to view everyday events and find some element of humor or meaning in them. He is a man who makes an art of being different. I look to my father for the unconventional viewpoint on things, and even though we disagree on some issues, I have always strived to live with one of his favorite expressions in mind: "Always give the benefit of the doubt. Always assume the best of people." He has said this to me many a time over the last three decades. The simple ideal represented is perhaps naive, but it helps counter the cynicism that is so easy to develop in life.

The most lacking part of my relationship with my father is the day-to-day living experience. When the household sepa-rated, my mother was given custody of the children, and my fa-ther ended up spending "special" time with the us. Dinners out, movies, special events—the time together became an occasion not unlike a date. Behaviors were better, interaction less honest. I find that it is tough to get to know someone if you don't have some basic data: what sort of cereal he eats, whether he is neat or messy, will he come home from work and watch the news be-fore he does anything else? In my case, it meant that my father and I did not really begin to know each other until I was in my early twenties.

But even before that, I knew how much influence he had in my being, above and beyond the half of my DNA he supplied.

I am told that each of us is the product of a mixture of genetics, environment, upbringing. The combination of all the diverse elements make for some package that we call, by name, "me." Over the years, friends have observed, "Oh, you have your mother's nose," and "You sound so much like your father when you speak" many times.

These comments often get me wondering about the broader issue of self. Who am I? Where do the parts of me come from? I am told that I think like my stepfather, but that I am wired up in the same squirrely way that my father is, in a blend of fathers that I find very satisfying. These men are my heroes, my mentors, my models, both good and bad.

When I realized that my father wasn't Saul Steinberg, I wasn't really disappointed. To this day, I cannot see anything by Steinberg without having an association with my father. It has a good feeling to it. In some way, the image still holds a small corner of my mind open with a label for my father that says "hero." And considering how my father and I fought when I was a teenager, having a small ember of the hero burning in preparation of a calmer time was a fine thing.

It is wrenching to have the object of one's adoration and the source of one's protection turn into an ogre, real or perceived. When I was small, my father was an all-powerful, all-knowing, and wonderful man, and because my frame of reference was so small, I could not conceive that he was a small part of an enormous whole. As a teen, I reversed myself, deciding that my father was hopelessly awful and stupid, a flat-out jerk.

I finally did grow up, and at some point the reality that my father is just a man who does the best he can sank in. If we are lucky, we will all learn to forgive our parents for being less than perfect, just as we hope that our own children will forgive us our human weaknesses.

When John died, I became the keeper of his ashes. In a dull brown plastic box, his remains sat on the top shelf of my closet for six years. That he stayed there for so long did not indicate disrespect. His death and arranging to cremate him was hard for us, especially my mother, and no one looked forward to finding him a burial plot. It just got put off. No one minded. They all knew where he was, and I was glad for the comfort that some part of him was right there in my home. When John's first grandchild was born, I held her up to his box of ashes and introduced him, knowing how pleased he would have been to have grandchildren. When my second child was born sick, I sat in that same closet and cried. I felt great comfort and strength in my memories of John.

On a snowy day in January, the family gathered at the cemetery, under a tall cedar. My daughter, just barely three, did not understand the solemnity of the moment, and as she was picking snowflakes off her great-grandmother's blue overcoat, she asked why we were here. I explained gently that we were burying her grandfather John. And she wanted to know why we were burying him. As I explained that John was dead, Sarah began to dance, running in circles around her grandmother, singing, "John is dead."

My first instinct was horror, that my child should be so insensitive to her grandmother's grief. I began to shush her, apologizing as I did, but my mother laughed and smiled around her tears, and allowed as it felt awfully good to have the lightness of heart from a small child just at that moment. John, she said, would have approved.

I set the box down in the casket, and watched as the gravedigger closed the lid and filled the hole in with earth. I finally said good-bye, re-experiencing the grief while reminding myself of the great joy that I had in knowing John. I stop every so often, and wonder what he would have said about some news item or event. I imagine his enthusiasm for life, and I feel glad.

To claim for fathers a philosopher, a scientist, and Saul Steinberg is a pretty fine heritage. My father lives for what may be possible in life, John lived for what may be possible in science, and Saul Steinberg lives for the silly fantasies a child may hold in his heart.

When I stop and consider the title of this story, I realize that it is incorrect. It should read "Like Fathers, Like Son."

Epilogue

Today, for me at least, is July 3, 1995. It is after eight in the evening, and I am sitting on the lanai (that means porch in Hawaiian) of a condominium on the west coast of Maui in the Hawaiian Islands. Being close to the equator, the sun has set earlier than I am used to, and it feels late. My children are fast asleep on the sofa bed just inside the screen door from where I sit, and my wife has given me a peck on the cheek as she herself calls it a night.

It is early here, but by our bodies' reckoning, it is well past eleven, and we've had a busy day. We went to the beach and swam and built sand castles and just generally ran around in circles.

It is catching up with me and I am feeling a bit on the groggy side. I am supposed to be on vacation at the moment. But here beside my lap top computer is a stack of stories to be looked at and edited, marked up, and printed out for the editor in New York. I feel some obligation to get one or two more done, even though I'd much rather look up and watch the stars rise over the Pacific Ocean and listen to the trade winds rustle the palm trees.

In all my life, I never imagined that I would be here now, doing this. Oh, yeah, imagining being on Maui takes no effort, but that I might be sitting here, typing these stories to an unseen audience, well I would not have guessed that one. I am trying to picture you now, sitting on your porches, reading in bed or a favorite chair, maybe on the train on your way into town. Perhaps one of you is sitting on the same lanai, having a cup of coffee. More than a few of you will be fathers as well.

In writing this book, I have done two things. One is that I have reexamined the concept of being a father. I have taken a very long and careful look at what it means, to me, and I have concluded that while I understand many of the fundamentals, it is still full of mystery and uncertainty. The second is that I have observed more of my own children and remembered more of my own childhood, living a blitz of experiences and memories simultaneously. I have filled copious notebooks, tapes, scrap paper, and the backs of business cards with all manner of ideas on the subject. Today, sitting at the beach, I jotted down one more event, to include here, to conclude the thoughts in this book.

Today, we went to a small beach just north of here to swim and snorkel. Sarah has spent every Friday of the last school year swimming with her class, and she has become quite the capable and confident swimmer. As soon as we arrived at the beach, she was searching the bags for her mask and fins and snorkel, ready to drag a parent out into the surf to see what we could see.

This was very much a replay of a previous trip here; the two of us swam out into ten- or twelve-foot-deep water, and watched the fish dart around, inspecting us for food, and then finning away sullenly when it became apparent that we were empty-handed. Sarah would shout at me around her snorkel, pointing out big fish and little ones, and then asking if we could go out farther.

But the basic difference was this time, she was swimming on her own. She did not need me there. Well, perhaps she did from the stand point that I was a form of insurance, to make sure she was okay. But like taking her first step, she has learned to swim and dive and float in the ocean, without needing a life ring or raft, and most important, without needing her father to hold onto.

I felt a mixture of great pride and great sadness as we worked our way back toward the beach. She was so excited, so thrilled with seeing the fish that she did not even note the passing of a mile stone. But I noticed, and I think her mother did, too. One more accomplishment in her life, one more thing we, her parents, have prodded her to do, and thereby we have moved her just a little further away from us.

I cannot dwell on this as too sad an event. My pride in my children is far too great to be sad for my diminishing importance as a father. And I realize that beyond everything else, this is my job. I told Sarah how proud I was of her, how impressed I was with her skills, thereby adding, I expect, a little more strength to her ability to break orbit from the home planet and fly off on her own.

Someday, my children will be grown and married and moved away, to have their own lives, families, and children. Perhaps they will fall into deep and dark pits along the way, and I will only have the memory of their childhood to sustain me. Perhaps they will be the envy of every other father on the face of the planet, held up as the best examples of what a fine thing it is to have children. There is no way of knowing. It's a crap shoot, and you have to hope that the subtle flick of your wrist as you launch the die, the guidance and wisdom and *love* you give your children along the path, will see all of you through.

My life as a father is built upon a foundation of hope for the best possible outcome.

But in the meantime, it is time for bed. The sun will be up early tomorrow and the chidren will rise with it, wondering when we are going to go to the beach. There are fishies to see and sand castles to be built.

About the Author

Hunter S. Fulghum is a telecommunications engineer in Seattle, where he was raised and now lives with his wife of twelve years, Marie, and their children, Sarah and Max.